956.7044
USC
CPS—MORRILL SCHOOL

Life of an American soldier in Iraq.

34880030035294

W9-BGU-490

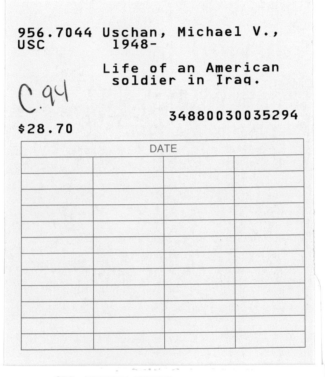

956.7044 Uschan, Michael V.,
USC   1948-

Life of an American
soldier in Iraq.

34880030035294

C.94

$28.70

DATE			

CPS—MORRILL SCHOOL
CHICAGO PUBLIC SCHOOLS
6011 S ROCKWELL STREET
CHICAGO, IL 60629
03/13/2006

BAKER & TAYLOR

956
45c
C. 94
200 6
$28.70

AMERICAN
WAR LIBRARY

★ The Iraq War ★

LIFE OF AN AMERICAN
SOLDIER IN IRAQ

AMERICAN
WAR LIBRARY

★ ★ ★ ★

★ The Iraq War ★

LIFE OF AN AMERICAN SOLDIER IN IRAQ

Titles in the American War Library series include:

The Iraq War
The Homefront
Life of an American Soldier in Iraq
Rebuilding Iraq
Weapons of War

The American Revolution

The Civil War

The Cold War

The Korean War

The Persian Gulf War

The Vietnam War

The War on Terrorism

World War I

World War II

AMERICAN WAR LIBRARY

★ ★ ★ ★

★ The Iraq War ★

LIFE OF AN AMERICAN SOLDIER IN IRAQ

by Michael V. Uschan

LUCENT BOOKS

An imprint of Thomson Gale, a part of The Thomson Corporation

THOMSON

★

GALE™

Detroit • New York • San Francisco • San Diego • New Haven, Conn. • Waterville, Maine • London • Munich

THOMSON

GALE

This book is dedicated to Staff Sergeant Mike Ashby, Major Paige Augustino, Journalist Second Class Farrukh Daniel, Sergeant Tim Hammond, Steelworker Third Class Paul Hartje, Construction Mechanic Second Class Gary Kernodle, Captain Tim Martz, Master Sergeant Marlin Mosley, and Master Sergeant Gregory Sielepkowski—for their service to their country in the Iraq War and for helping with this book. Thank you!

© 2005 Thomson Gale, a part of the Thomson Corporation.

Thomson and Star Logo are trademarks and Gale and Lucent Books are registered trademarks used herein under license.

For more information, contact
Lucent Books
27500 Drake Rd.
Farmington Hills, MI 48331-3535
Or you can visit our Internet site at http://www.gale.com

ALL RIGHTS RESERVED.
No part of this work covered by the copyright hereon may be reproduced or used in any form or by any means—graphic, electronic, or mechanical, including photocopying, recording, taping, Web distribution, or information storage retrieval systems—without the written permission of the publisher.

Every effort has been made to trace the owners of copyrighted material.

LIBRARY OF CONGRESS CATALOGING-IN-PUBLICATION DATA

Uschan, Michael V., 1948–
   Life of an American soldier in Iraq / by Michael V. Uschan.
     p. cm. — (American war library)
   Includes bibliographical references and index.
   ISBN 1-59018-541-2 (hard cover : alk. paper)
   1. Iraq War, 2003—Personal narratives, American—Juvenile literature. I. Title. II. Series:
American war library. Persian Gulf.
   DS79.763.U83 2004
   956.7044'34'092273—dc22
                                                     2004010370

Printed in the United States of America

✫ Contents ✫

A Nation Forged by War

The United States, like many nations, was forged and defined by war. Despite Benjamin Franklin's opinion that "There never was a good war or a bad peace," the United States owes its very existence to the War of Independence, one to which Franklin wholeheartedly subscribed. The country forged by war in 1776 was tempered and made stronger by the Civil War in the 1860s.

The Texas Revolution, the Mexican-American War, and the Spanish-American War expanded the country's borders and gave it overseas possessions. These wars made the United States a world power, but this status came with a price, as the nation became a key but reluctant player in both World War I and World War II.

Each successive war further defined the country's role on the world stage. Following World War II, U.S. foreign policy redefined itself to focus on the role of defender, not only of the freedom of its own citizens, but also of the freedom of people everywhere. During the Cold War that followed World War II until the collapse of the Soviet Union, defending the world meant fighting communism. This goal, manifested in the Korean and Vietnam conflicts, proved elusive, and soured the American public on its achievability. As the United States emerged as the world's sole superpower, American foreign policy has been guided less by national interest and more by protecting international human rights. But as involvement in Somalia and Kosovo prove, this goal has been equally elusive.

As a result, the country's view of itself changed. Bolstered by victories in World Wars I and II, Americans first relished the role of protector. But, as war followed war in a seemingly endless procession, Americans began to doubt their leaders, their motives, and themselves. The Vietnam War especially caused people to question the validity of sending its young people to die in places where they were not particularly wanted and for people who did not seem especially grateful.

While the most obvious changes brought about by America's wars have been geopolitical in nature, many other aspects of society have been touched. War often does not bring about change directly, but acts instead like the catalyst in a chemical reaction, accelerating changes already in progress.

Some of these changes have been societal. The role of women in the United States had been slowly changing, but World War II put thousands into the workforce and into uniform. They might have gone back to being housewives after the war, but equality, once experienced, would not be forgotten.

Likewise, wars have accelerated technological change. The necessity for faster airplanes and more destructive bombs led to the development of jet planes and nuclear energy. Artificial fibers developed for parachutes in the 1940s were used in clothing of the 1950s.

Lucent Books' American War Library covers key wars in the development of the nation. Each war is covered in several volumes, to allow for more detail, context, and to provide volumes on often neglected subjects, such as the kamikazes of World War II, or the weapons used in the Civil War. As with all Lucent books, notes, annotated bibliographies, and appendixes such as glossaries give students a launching point for further research. In addition, sidebars and archival photographs enhance the text. Together, each volume in The American War Library will aid students in understanding how America's wars have shaped and changed its politics, economics, and society.

Why They Were There

November 11 is Veterans Day, a holiday that honors Americans who fought for their country. On that date in 2003, Lieutenant General Ricardo Sanchez opened his news conference in Baghdad with an emotional tribute to the men and women who had fought in the Iraq War to topple the brutal regime of Saddam Hussein and who were still working months later to help Iraqis forge a brighter future for their nation. Said Sanchez:

As many of you know, today has special meaning for those of us in uniform. Veterans Day is the day that we honor and remember those brave heroes who have defended the causes of freedom and liberty throughout the world. As the commander of the military here in Iraq, I would like to personally salute our magnificent soldiers, sailors, airmen, [and] Marines as they continue in this proud tradition of service. They are today's veterans. Their valor and professionalism is honorable. I'm fiercely proud to lead these fine men and women. They deserve our highest respect and our admiration. They are all heroes.[1]

For the tens of thousands of armed forces personnel still stationed in Iraq, as well as for those who had already returned home, Veterans Day 2003—and all those that would follow in the future—held new meaning for them because of what they had experienced. One of those freshly minted veterans was Major Paige Augustino of the Wisconsin Air National Guard's 128th Air Refueling Wing. After piloting a giant tanker plane to refuel fighter jets high above Iraq during combat in March and April of 2003, Augustino flew back to her base in Milwaukee with a deep and lasting sense of accomplishment. She described her feelings upon returning home: "You're very proud. It's kind of euphoric when you come home. You know that you changed history, you've altered the course of history. And what you've done is going to affect the entire world for years to come."[2]

That feeling was shared by hundreds of thousands of soldiers who had done their duty for their country in Operation Iraqi Freedom, the U.S. military name for the Iraq War. Yet the reasons why the men and women who served in Iraq had decided to join their nation's armed forces in the first place were all different.

Why They Enlisted

Unlike some periods in U.S. history when the federal government drafted citizens, today every member of the U.S. military voluntarily joins. And all those who fought in Iraq had their own individual reasons for enlisting.

One of hundreds of thousands of U.S. soldiers who served in the Iraq War, a sailor is welcomed home in November 2003.

As for many other soldiers, it was the promise of adventure that led Julia Fadell to join the army. When she finished high school, Fadell wanted to travel and "to do something different and not get caught in a routine job."[3] The military fulfilled her wishes. During the next two decades she lived in Panama, Japan, Alaska, and Kuwait, performing a wide variety of jobs while serving in the army and army reserve, the branch of the military whose personnel serve part-time but are called up for full-time active duty when they are needed.

In April 2003 Fadell, now a sergeant as well as a mother of six children ranging in age from six to twenty-two, was sent to Iraq with the U.S. Army Reserve's 257th Transportation Company. Fadell drove a forty-ton truck, delivering supplies and hauling heavy equipment. Although she came under fire and deeply missed her husband and children, she loved the experience. "I wouldn't want to have missed out on this. Every day's an adventure,"[4] she said after having served there for almost six months.

First Lieutenant Jersey Matyszczuk was one of many U.S. soldiers born in foreign nations who had grown to love America so much that they joined the military to fight for their adopted country. Matyszczuk had emigrated to New York City from his native Poland in the 1990s. He enlisted in the army because he was grateful for his new life in America. "I owe something to this country. And this is a way of paying it back,"[5] the Third Infantry officer said in Kuwait while waiting for the war to begin.

For some soldiers, the terrorist attacks of September 11, 2001, were the catalyst to join the military. The death and destruction that resulted when terrorists crashed airplanes into the World Trade Center in New York City and the Pentagon in Washington, D.C., killing several thousand people, made them want to defend America against future aggression. Robert Schiria was one American who enlisted out of anger over the attacks. "It killed me to see something like that happen in our country," said Schiria. "[I] just sat down and said, 'This is what [I'm] going to do.'"[6]

Schiria's comments came in November 2003 while he was recuperating in an army hospital in Iraq from back and leg injuries. He was injured when a grenade struck the armored vehicle he was driving in Baghdad. But Schiria said that even if he had known he would be wounded, he would still have enlisted: "I would still definitely be here. This is what I signed up for."[7]

Still others enlist in the armed forces hoping to achieve recognition and challenge themselves. Army staff sergeant Richard Bear's trip to Iraq to fight with the Eighty-second Airborne Division began in this way. Bear said he was motivated to enlist by the reception U.S. soldiers received when they came back from the first Iraq War in 1991:

Right after the first Gulf War, . . . I saw a busful of reservists returning home. People were clapping and cheering and honking their horns. These guys were heroes. I thought to myself, "That's what I want—recognition, a sense of accomplishment."[8]

Soldiers Won the War

A study by the U.S. Army War College's Strategic Studies Institute in September 2003 titled "Why They Fight: Combat Motivation in the Iraq War" argues that America's victory in the war was due more to the bravery and skill of its individual soldiers than to the superior weapons they employed, such as jet bombers, guided missiles, and tanks. Researchers who interviewed soldiers to assess how they fought claimed the key factor in winning the war was what is known as human power, or the sheer skill of soldiers. According to the study:

With the recent lightning swift combat successes of Operation IRAQI FREE-DOM, there may be a tendency to view with awe the lethality of U.S. technology and training. Indeed, the U.S. military is unmatched in the raw combat power it is capable of unleashing in a conflict. . . . However, . . . the true strength of America's military might lies not in its hardware or high-tech equipment, but in its soldiers.[9]

The study focused on the experience of ground troops. But its claim that the men and women who served in Iraq deserve credit for the victory holds true no matter whether they fought on land, in the air, or by sea, and whether they engaged the enemy at close quarters, from planes thousands of feet in the air, or aboard ships many miles away. It was the human power unleashed by members of every branch of the nation's armed forces that won the Iraq War.

Chapter 1

Preparing for War

In the first week of January 2003, when Sergeant Kenneth Forbes left for Iraq from Hunter Army Airfield in Savannah, Georgia, the sad farewells between loved ones and departing soldiers stirred up memories of a similar scene years earlier. In 1991, the eleven-year-old Forbes had waved goodbye to his dad, who was leaving to fight in the Middle East. A decade later Forbes could proudly say, "My father was in the [first] Gulf War, and I saw him leave. So now I'm in his shoes. I get to go finish what he began. It's awesome."[10]

Although the Iraq War did not begin until March 20, 2003, Forbes and some 200,000 other U.S. troops began assembling in Kuwait months earlier. This buildup was a massive, complex undertaking, one that required as much work as the war that would follow. In late 2002 and early 2003, U.S. soldiers began arriving in the Middle East by plane and ship. Most went to Kuwait, which borders Iraq, but some soldiers were also quartered in neighboring countries such as Saudi Arabia.

Simply getting soldiers to the war region was a huge undertaking. In late January 2003 when Colonel Louis Weber headed up the transfer of the army's Third Infantry to Iraq from Georgia, he tried to describe how tough the task was. "Try to imagine having 20,000 soldiers pick up and move out in a three week period. It's a lot more complicated than it looks,"[11] he admitted. In addition to getting his soldiers overseas, Weber and other military commanders had to make sure they took everything they needed to fight. As military personnel flowed into the region, an even more massive and steady stream of supplies arrived with them. Weapons they would use in battle were shipped—everything from rifles and bullets to tanks and helicopters. Tons of other cargo arriving daily at seaports and airfields included food, medical supplies, and tens of thousands of tents to house soldiers and their supplies.

Soldiers Are Called Up

In 2001 when U.S. officials had begun planning for a possible war in Iraq, one of their

Pep Talk from a General

Just as coaches often give athletes a pep talk before a big game, so do military leaders. In March 2003 Marine major general J.N. Mattis issued a stirring message to his soldiers before the start of the Iraq War. His words of advice and instructions on how to fight honorably were quoted in *The March Up: Taking Baghdad with the 1st Marine Division,* by Bing West and Ray L. Smith.

Chemical attack, treachery, and use of the innocent as human shields can be expected, as can other unethical tactics. Take it all in stride. Be the hunter, not the hunted; never allow your unit to be caught with its guard down. Use good judgment and act in the best interests of our Nation. You are part of the world's most feared and trusted force. Engage your brain before you engage your weapon. Share your courage with each other as we enter the uncertain terrain north of the [border between Kuwait and Iraq]. Keep faith in your comrades on your left and right and Marine Air overhead. Fight with a happy heart and strong spirit. For the mission's sake, for our country's sake, and the sake of the men who carried the Division's color in past battles—*who fought for life and never lost their nerve*—carry out your mission and *keep your honor clean.* Demonstrate to the world there is "No Better Friend, No Worse Enemy" than a U.S. Marine.

hardest tasks was deciding on the makeup of the armed force they would need to win. This involved deciding not only how many soldiers would be required but what kind of skills they would have to have. Military planners calculated how many soldiers were needed for actual combat, from bomber pilots to tank drivers, as well as the number of troops needed in support positions, such as cooks, doctors, and nurses.

Once the plans were drawn up, officials issued orders to military units with soldiers who had the skills required to carry out the war strategy. The majority of U.S. military personnel sent to Iraq were members of the nation's active duty armed forces, which then numbered about 1.4 million men and women in the army, air force, marines, and navy. But the federal government also called up nearly 190,000 personnel in reserve branches of various services as well as army and air National Guard units, military units which are organized by each state. Unlike full-time active duty military personnel, reserve and guard members normally train one weekend a month and for one extended two-week period each year, usually in the summer, to keep their military skills sharp in case they are needed. Now was such a time.

Thus for Major Paul Moffett, the Iraq War began in the summer of 2002 with a telephone call from his Tennessee National Guard office in Fayetteville notifying him that his unit was being activated to full-time duty. When Moffett hung up, he told other guardsmen about the orders: "I looked them dead in the eyes and said 'Boys, we've got the word. We're being mobilized.' They knew I wasn't joking." [12]

The phone calls like the one Moffett got meant that part-time soldiers living in communities across America would now become full-time soldiers. They would have to leave their civilian jobs and families and travel to a duty post in the United States or overseas to fulfill their mission in the war. Although most would be stationed in Iraq, others were sent to bases in other countries. Some soldiers were also assigned to bases located in the United States to perform the duties of soldiers who had been sent to war. Suddenly, people who worked as teachers, policemen, bankers, factory workers, small business owners, and even ministers donned military uniforms and became bomber pilots, truck drivers, and military policemen.

Before they could leave for the war, all the soldiers had to wrap up the loose ends of the lives they were leaving behind for up to a year (approximately the longest period they would be away from home). They had to deal with bills that would come due while they were gone, end apartment leases, find a place to store automobiles or other possessions, and make a host of other personal arrangements.

Sad Farewells

Most soldiers going off to war, however, found that the hardest part of leaving was saying good-bye to loved ones. Colonel Louis Weber explained that this is always difficult because neither the soldier nor his or her family knows what the future will bring. Said Weber about traveling into an unknown future, "Your kids ask, 'How long will you be gone, Daddy?' And you say, I don't know. 'Will you have to kill anybody?' I don't know. 'Will you go to Iraq?' Dunno. And all that uncer-

tainty weighs on you. In a deployment like this, you just don't know."[13]

Indeed, such open-ended deployments made many families' good-byes very emotional. In early January 2003 when four thousand marines and sailors left San Diego, California, on the USS *Tarawa*, wives, husbands, children, parents, and friends waved tearful good-byes. Said Corporal Rafael Avalos, "It's hard every time. It never gets easier."[14]

As difficult as it was for husbands and wives to say good-bye to each other, it was perhaps even harder for soldiers who had to leave children behind. And in the Iraq War, compared with other U.S. conflicts, a higher percentage of soldiers were parents. In 2003 roughly half of U.S. soldiers were married and had children, and 8 percent were single parents, figures that had doubled since the Gulf War in 1991.

Typical of this kind of separation was that endured by Lieutenant Colonel Jim Richardson and Lieutenant Colonel Laura Richardson, both of whom were army helicopter pilots. Before leaving for Iraq the Richardsons had to make living arrangements for Lauren, their fourteen-year-old daughter. She would stay with a friend during the school year at Fort Campbell in Kentucky and spend the summer with grandparents. Laura Richardson, who displays pictures of her family in the cockpit of her helicopter, worried more about her daughter's future than her own in facing combat: "The hardest thing about any deployment to the Gulf will be leaving her."[15] The Richardsons, however, would remain together during the war because they flew in the same unit.

The sad farewells that soldiers and their friends and families had to make when they departed for Iraq would continue throughout 2003 and into 2004. As soldiers in late 2003 and early 2004 reached the end of their deployment—the length of time they had to serve in Iraq—others were ordered overseas to take their place. The greatest number of these emotional farewells, however, occurred in the few months before the war began, as the United States massed tens of thousands of soldiers overseas for the coming battle in Iraq.

A Gathering for War

Before the war buildup began in late 2002, the air force and navy already had bases in countries near Iraq such as Saudi Arabia, Bahrain, and Kuwait. But in early 2003, even while negotiations continued with Saddam Hussein to forge a peaceful resolution to the differences between the two countries, the United States was building new military sites to house the increasing number of its soldiers in the region. By early February there were over 100,000 U.S. troops in Kuwait, with more arriving every day, along with tons of supplies.

It was a tremendously difficult task to move all the soldiers and equipment needed for the Iraq War. Most of the troops and supplies were carried to Persian Gulf ports in Kuwait by hundreds of ships. Some of these were U.S. Navy ships; others were civilian merchant ships the military hired to help with the war effort. The ships transported tanks, armored trucks, artillery pieces, rifles,

grenades, and other weapons. They also brought in a flood of supplies, everything from food for soldiers to portable hospitals that would treat the wounded. They even imported giant sections of steel bridges the infantry could use to rebuild structures that would inevitably be destroyed during the fighting. Some units required so much equipment that it took several ships to haul it all to the war zone. For example, six ships were used to bring in the 260 helicopters and 5,800 vehicles such as heavy trucks and oil tankers that the 20,000 soldiers of the 101st Airborne Division needed to fight in the war.

Supplies needed by the 101st and other units were taken off the ships at several ports. They were then delivered by truck to temporary staging areas in the Kuwaiti desert near the Iraqi border. These areas were given names like Camp Udairi, Camp Virginia, and Camp Doha. These camps housed the soldiers and their equipment for weeks and even several months. Naval reservist Paul Hartje, who helped haul equipment to the desert bases, claimed there was a lot of hard work involved in getting the camps ready: "We were pretty busy establishing camps for incoming army [personnel], working sixteen-hour days. We were running supplies to the border [with Iraq] for the initial push [the first drive into Iraq to start the war]. We were transporting [food], water, just extra supplies to keep everyone going."[16]

Some of the supplies were delivered by hundreds of planes, which would also be

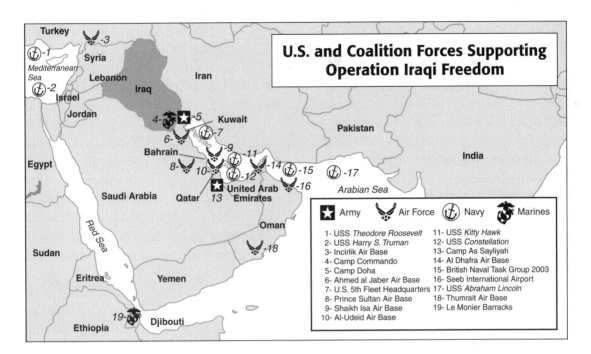

used in combat. Simply gathering so many planes in one place was a difficult task. While hundreds of planes were flying into bases around Iraq, the navy was also helping planes land. Three battle groups were moved into the Persian Gulf and two into the Mediterranean Sea. Each group was centered around an aircraft carrier, a giant ship that launches airplanes. The groups also included six to eight support vessels that perform various tasks, including protecting ships from possible attack.

Not Like Home

As the American force in the region grew larger, tent cities sprang up in the middle of the desert, which soldiers soon began calling "the sandbox." Living conditions were basic, with few frills. Soldiers slept on cots in tents or sometimes outdoors in sleeping bags. They usually had portable toilets but occasionally had to use trenches dug in the sand. They sweltered in desert heat without air conditioning—the temperature in March was already in the 90s—and there was usually not enough water to take a shower.

Another inconvenience in many prewar camps was a lack of decent food—many were not big enough to have their own cooking and dining facilities. Thus soldiers often had nothing to eat but army-rationed meals ready to eat (MREs). Many soldiers found MREs unappetizing and jokingly referred to them as "meals rejected by everybody." That is why soldiers at Camp Coyote loved the call of "Hot chow, hot chow"—it meant they would get a hot meal instead of an MRE. The savior for those marines was Lance Corporal

Timothy-Ryan Gaball, who brought the food to them in a truck from nearby Camp Saipan, which was larger and better equipped. According to Master Sergeant Michael J. Levinson, "My devil dogs [marines] look forward each day to Gaball coming out to bring them chow."[17]

Although the camps were primitive, Major Michael Yaroma said conditions at Camp Saipan, named after a famed World War II battle (as were many others), were acceptable. "Relatively speaking [they] aren't that bad. But everybody is away from their family, and that hurts,"[18] he explained. Forced separation from family and friends made the desert outposts seem even more desolate and lonely. Soldiers could only occasionally transmit an e-mail or make a telephone call, so mail was the main way they kept in touch with home. Receiving mail was a huge morale booster, although it took two or three weeks for letters to be delivered.

The tens of thousands of soldiers, sailors, and fliers who were gathering for war, however, usually did not have much time to think too long about being lonely or about how uncomfortable living conditions were. They were too busy preparing for the job they had come to do.

A Long Wait

Until the war began, officers kept the soldiers busy training and preparing to fight with drills that would hone their combat skills. Infantry soldiers stationed in Kuwait had huge areas in which to practice how to live and fight in desert conditions, and they took advantage of this. They practiced moving in formation in the desert's shifting sands and learned how to keep their weapons from being clogged by grains of sand. Gradually, they became acclimated to the conditions they would be fighting in. Soldiers also learned basic commands in Arabic, such as the words for "do not resist." They knew they would need such phrases to communicate with the Iraqi soldiers they expected to capture.

The Kuwaiti Crud

Although its name sounds like a joke, the "Kuwaiti crud" was not funny for military personnel in Kuwait. It refers to respiratory problems soldiers experienced because there was so much dust in the air, far more than they were accustomed to breathing in. This excerpt from a story titled, "Mideast Notebook: Colds, J-Lo Rumor Distress Troops" found in the March 15, 2003, edition of *Stars and Stripes* explains this very real ailment.

At night in the sleeping tents of Camp Udairi, Kuwait, there is more to hear than the soft snoring of service members. Cough, cough. Hack, hack. It's the sound of what troops call the "Kuwaiti crud"—the mild respiratory distress that comes with breathing in dust 24 hours a day for weeks on end.... [It] is like a low-grade cold [followed] by a slightly runny nose and a deep cough from the chest. It causes little trouble during the day but can be torture at night, when the coughing and hacking can keep troops, and their healthy tentmates, from getting much sleep.

Training, however, could be tedious and repetitive. Marine Chris Secondino admitted he grew tired of one particular task. "The worst," he said, "is when you dig a hole and then have to fill it, and then they take you back to the same place to dig another one. I'll tell you what, I can certainly dig a good hole now."[19] The job was not as meaningless as it sounds—digging holes was necessary to secure the artillery piece Secondino helped fire. Artillery crews also endured tedious drills. They practiced moving, loading, and firing their guns at night in the dark to avoid detection by the enemy.

In the weeks before the war began, there were many ways that the military prepared for battle. While sailors on board aircraft carriers assembled bombs, pilots flew over Iraq to acquaint themselves with targets they would soon be ordered to strike. And everyone worked on readying the weapons they would fight with, from rifles to high-tech computer systems that would fire missiles at targets hundreds of miles away.

Some of the preparation was fun. For example, tank crews enjoyed the lighthearted job of naming their vehicles. Soldiers came up with names like "Big Punisher" and "Baghdad Bound," named for the Iraqi capital, which was their ultimate destination.

An artillery specialist adjusts the barrel of a .50 caliber machine gun. Artillery crews participated in numerous drills to prepare for combat.

Prewar Boredom

For most soldiers, that journey to Baghdad could not come soon enough. Even though they were working long hours training and preparing to fight, they were becoming increasingly bored while waiting for the war to begin.

The problem was that, aside from training, soldiers stuck in the middle of a desert had almost nothing to do. One of the few activities available was reading, and soldiers tried to make magazines or books last as long as possible. Chief Warrant Officer Kurt Westrum, for example, read and reread a magazine with a picture of Christina Aguilera on its cover. "I read this thing from front to back and it takes about three hours,"[20] he said. This was precious time in which soldiers could escape mentally from the boredom of camp life.

Another way soldiers entertained themselves was to make up amusing stories. It was common for them to spread harmless rumors, such as that stars like Jennifer Lopez or Kid Rock were going to visit and put on a show. Even though most of the rumors seemed unbelievable, soldiers enjoyed them because they took their minds off the dull routine that surrounded them.

Sporting activities were another good way to pass the time, but soldiers had to choose games that suited their environment. Infantry soldiers, for example, could play tackle football in the sand, but sailors aboard the USS *Abraham Lincoln,* a carrier anchored in the Persian Gulf, had to be content with tossing a football beneath the shadows of the jet fighter planes they were readying to attack Iraq. Some sailors even practiced golf by whacking golf balls into the ocean off the carrier's huge flight deck.

Marines at Camp Coyote held what they called a rodeo field meet. One of the meet's events was a relay, a contest in which teams of eight marines pushed a Humvee (a military vehicle) weighing over one ton through the sand. They also competed in the "dizzy-izzy," in which they spun around a pole to make themselves dizzy and then tried to run back to their group to tag the next marine in line. The soldiers were so disoriented that they had trouble running and sometimes fell down. Even though it made him look silly to the soldiers he commanded, Colonel Dave G. Reist participated. He knew the event was not about competition but about having fun and building camaraderie. This sentiment was shared by Lance Corporal Michael K. Casey, who said, "I think it brought us closer as a unit as well as being fun."[21]

Precombat Nerves

Although such activities may seem silly, the soldiers desperately needed this escape from the reality of the coming war. They knew that when combat began, they could all be injured or killed. In the weeks and months in which the soldiers had to wait for the war to begin, many became restless and anxious.

Even the uncertainty of when the war would start began to unsettle many soldiers. In fact, because talks were still going on between the United States and Iraq to resolve their problems, no one knew if there would even be a war or if the situation would be resolved peacefully. This made many soldiers impatient. As Joseph Scully of the Third Infantry Division admitted, "I'm tired of sitting here and listening to all this politics on the radio."[22] It was a sentiment shared by many others who had been assembled for war. Navy journalist Farrukh Daniel, who had been in Iraq since late January 2003 writing articles documenting the buildup, explained that the uncertainty was troubling: "You're alone, you've left your family, you're in a pretty desolate place, and you don't know what's going to happen."[23]

On the eve of war, some soldiers were also worried about what would happen in combat. Almost every soldier in history has carried some fear into battle, and they all had to learn how to deal with their fear so it did not overcome them during battle. For example, although marine David Grubb understood that he might be scared when the time came to fire his shoulder-mounted rocket launcher against the enemy, the weapons specialist said the fact that he might be afraid was not important. "What I do with the fear," he said, "determines whether the fear is a good thing or a bad thing. If I let the fear overcome me, that's a bad thing. If I use fear as courage, that's a good thing."[24]

Like other soldiers heading into combat before them in wars throughout history, many turned to God as a source of strength to prepare for the difficult test facing them. In desert camps throughout Kuwait, military chaplains baptized many soldiers in makeshift, bathtub-sized holes dug into the sand and lined with plastic to hold water. Many more soldiers attended services or prayed on their own.

Although the comfort of religion would help many soldiers ease their fears of combat, it was still hard to prepare psychologically for battle. The thought that they might have to kill someone in combat or that they could be killed themselves was unsettling. For most soldiers, combat would be as much a battle with themselves as a battle with the enemy. Although they would have to fight enemy soldiers physically, they would have to conquer their own emotions first so they could perform their job well. A day before the war began, Lieutenant Mike Washburn summed up the inner struggle he faced while waiting for war: "It may be bad. It may be ugly. I may regret the day that I ever came here, but unless we go, I'll never know if I can stand that ultimate test. This is the ultimate challenge for me, to lead a platoon into battle."[25]

The need to do their job, no matter what, was reinforced for some soldiers in a

Drills to Stay Alive

Before the war began, marines at Camp Coyote in Kuwait worked to keep their battle skills sharp. Such efforts were vital because the soldiers had to learn how to fight in a desert environment, which was a new challenge to most marines. Groups of soldiers had to learn how to travel together across the wide open desert terrain without breaking their battle formations. And because the howling desert winds could at times make verbal communication between soldiers difficult, they had to practice other methods of communication.

In a story in the military newspaper *Stars and Stripes,* Corporal Jose Cervantes explained that the drills also built trust and support among the soldiers: "It's building confidence in the junior Marines that they're doing what they're supposed to be doing. . . . Out here, it's our lives we're talking about. We have our lives in each other's hands."

ceremony in a camp in Kuwait on March 12, 2003, in which they repeated their soldiers' oath to "support and defend the Constitution of the United States against all enemies, foreign and domestic." Afterward, Lieutenant Colonel Eric Schwartz said the seven hundred soldiers he commanded "are at the defining moment" of their lives and that the ceremony meant a great deal to them. "This was a lot more serious than a pre-game pep talk," he said. "This was more internal, more personal for these soldiers."[26]

War at Last

The chance to prove themselves finally came on March 20, 2003. For soldiers of the U.S. Army's Twelfth Aviation Brigade, the conflict began when their camp was fired on by Iraqi missiles. When the attack ended, Sergeant Cyndee Carnes barked out words that explained how their lives had all changed: "This is the real live stuff ladies [her joking term for the men and women she commanded]. If we weren't soldiers a few minutes ago, we are now."[27]

Chapter 2

Fighting from a Distance: The Air Force and Navy

In the early morning darkness of March 20, 2003, Navy lieutenant Roderick Kurtz was one of the first pilots to bomb Iraq. When Kurtz landed on the aircraft carrier USS *Abraham Lincoln* after participating in one of the largest and most powerful aerial attacks in military history, he stated simply, "We started a pretty big fight out there."[28] Navy captain Mark Fox, who commanded planes launched from the USS *Constellation*, said his first mission in the war seemed very dramatic. Fox was fascinated by the antiaircraft fire and surface-to-air missiles aimed at his plane, which exploded brilliantly when they missed and lit up the ink-black predawn sky. He compared the intense flashing to a sporting event with "people snapping flash bulbs all over the stadium. That's what it was like. It was a visceral event."[29]

In the massive aerial assault, fighter jets, bombers, and other aircraft that took off from land bases scattered around the Middle East and Mediterranean Sea area joined hundreds of planes launched from carriers.

Scores of missiles that could strike targets a thousand miles away were also launched from submarines and other ships. As the first flight of thirteen missiles left the USS *Bunker Hill,* Lieutenant Commander Curtis Goodnight bid them farewell with a quiet "Happy trails."[30]

The U.S. Air Force and Navy began the Iraq War by unleashing immense firepower. Bombs and missiles rained down destructively on targets throughout Iraq in the war's initial offensive, which had been nicknamed "shock and awe." But even though people around the world were awed when they read stories or viewed film of the damage the strike caused, those who powered it were not. Said Ted Nelson, a sailor aboard the *Abraham Lincoln,* "The 'shock and awe' thing—everybody was amazed for about five minutes [and] then they went back to work."[31] Indeed, the men and women who served in the navy and air force were simply doing the job for which they had been trained. Interestingly, the Iraq War they would experience was quite different from the one fought by soldiers on land.

A Different Type of War

Although the navy and air force personnel who fought in Iraq worked incredibly hard, in many ways they had an easier time than ground troops. When pilots flew back to their bases or aircraft carriers, they were no longer in constant danger of being killed because the war was usually quite far from their ships. Their living conditions were also much better than those of infantry soldiers invading Iraq. They generally ate hot meals, could take showers and sleep in beds, and had at least some communication with friends and family through telephones and computers. Indeed, Rosa Diaz, a sixteen-year navy veteran who served on the USS *Rainier,* was able to regularly send e-mails to her three children. According to Diaz, "My two younger kids are

having a hard time, but we e-mail a lot back and forth. They need a lot of reassurance just to let them know that I'll be all right." [32]

Another significant difference was that most navy and air force personnel served in the war for a shorter period of time. Many were able to head home after only a few months because they had successfully accomplished their mission, which was to weaken Iraq's military defenses in the first stage of the conflict. By the time President George W. Bush declared on May 1, 2003, that major combat in the war had ended, most of the planes and ships that participated had already headed home or were preparing to leave Iraq.

Most notably, sailors and fliers in the Iraq War did not have a close-up view of its death and destruction. Pilots that dropped bombs on Iraq flew thousands of feet above their targets; the powerful explosions they created far below were nearly invisible to their naked eye. Likewise, weapons technicians who fired missiles from ships hundreds of miles away had no visual contact with their targets.

This long-distance aspect of the war led many sailors and pilots to feel detached about what they were doing. For example, after pressing the button to fire missiles from a ship floating thirty miles off the Iraqi coast, Petty Officer Clayton Bartels admitted that he did not dwell on the consequences of his action. Said Bartels, "I am not paid to philosophize. I don't usually worry about it. But if I wanted to find out where the missiles have hit, I could." [33] After returning to the *Abraham Lincoln* following a bombing run in early

---

An Important Target

During the Iraq War, Lieutenant Colonel Frank Swan was a weapon systems officer on a B-1 bomber that received orders to attack a high-ranking official on the ground. Swan described the excitement on board his plane in a U.S. Defense Department transcript.

> You get kind of an adrenaline rush, the crew does, but then you fall back to your original training that says, "Hey, let's get the job done." And we knew we had to react quickly. . . . We really didn't have time to reflect on anything. . . . Everything went as advertised; the weapons came off [that is, were deployed]. . . . You just fall totally into the execute mode and kill the target.

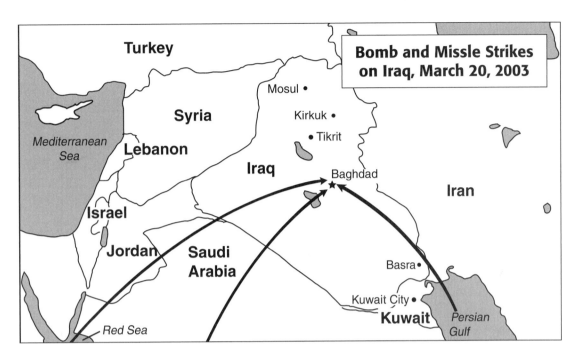

Bomb and Missle Strikes on Iraq, March 20, 2003

April, Lieutenant Stan Wilson described a similar sense of detachment from the war. However, Wilson admitted that even though he and other pilots did not have a close-up view of the damage they caused, they internalized the end result of their missions. "We know we're killing people [but] we don't talk about it, don't worry about it,"[34] he said.

Air Bases and Sorties

In that first night of "shock and awe," air force and navy planes flew about two thousand sorties, the military term for a combat flight. Hundreds of planes were launched from aircraft carriers floating far from the sites being attacked. The navy pilots sometimes had to fly several hundred miles to reach their targets. Many air force planes had even longer routes to the battle zone, with some B-2

bombers coming all the way from Whiteman Air Force Base in Missouri. Other flights originated in the Indian Ocean and England or from some thirty bases in the Middle East and Mediterranean.

Thus the air force personnel who fought in the Iraq War were usually housed far from the actual war zone. This gave them a greater degree of safety and better living conditions than those of infantry soldiers fighting on the ground in Iraq. Nevertheless, air force accommodations could also leave much to be desired. Major Paige Augustino, a tanker plane pilot, said the base she flew out of was a rundown military site that had been condemned. Interviewed in November 2003, Augustino said conditions there were so bad that it was hard to sleep, even though she was exhausted by sixteen-hour days. Said Augustino:

We were actually pulled out of one place that was fairly decent and then housed in condemned buildings. Disgusting, nasty, tiny little beds infested with bugs. Holes in the walls. No screens on the window; the mosquitoes were terrible. For us it was bad. It was very difficult to get the proper rest. We were pretty burned out by the time it was over.[35]

Some fliers who attacked Iraq, however, never had to give up the comforts of home. In mid-April, Captain Brian Gallo and Captain Brian Bogue flew a B-2 bomber on a seven-thousand-mile round trip. They went from Whiteman Air Force Base to Iraq and dropped sixteen bombs. Then they turned around and flew home. Their mission lasted thirty-seven hours and for the most part was so uneventful that they worked on crossword puzzles during the flight to stay alert.

When they arrived at their target, Bogue admitted it felt strange to have flown to Iraq so quickly: "I couldn't believe it. It is so weird. I had taken off from the middle of Missouri and now I'm in the middle of a country in the Mideast." The feeling of returning home just as swiftly after their brief trip to the war zone was no less bizarre. While watching news about the fighting with his wife the night he got back, Gallo reflected on his incredible journey: "It was kind of surreal. Just [hours] ago I was involved in this and now I'm on the La-Z-Boy watching TV."[36]

Refueling

Gallo and Bogue could never have flown their astonishing mission without being able to refuel five times while en route. They did this using huge tanker planes that refuel aircraft while they are flying. By mid-April when the air attack was beginning to wind down, tankers had flown more than seventy-five

Women in the Iraq War

During the Iraq War, Air Force major Paige Augustino piloted a huge tanker plane that refueled fighter and bomber jets in midair so they could continue their missions. For Augustino, one of the most interesting moments of the war came when she refueled a jet fighter and discovered that the plane's pilot was also a woman. She talked about the meeting in an interview with the author.

When you make your connection [with the receiving plane], the conversation goes between both airplanes. It kind of took me [by surprise] when the pilot connected and she made her check-in. It's like, "Oh, wait a second, we've got a woman fighter pilot back there." That was kind of interesting. I thought to myself that it was good to see how the military has come around 180 degrees from the past [when women pilots were not allowed in combat], that today you had a female tanker pilot refueling a female fighter pilot in a war zone. Back ten, fifteen years ago, that was completely unheard of. It's nice to see that the women who came before us and fought so hard and pioneered, that their efforts didn't fall [by] the wayside.

hundred sorties and delivered more than 46 million gallons of fuel.

The rendezvous between tanker planes and the smaller fighters and bombers is a delicate ballet, one that takes place tens of thousands of feet in the air at 300 miles per hour. Some of these tankers are monstrous; for example, the KC-135R Stratotanker is 136 feet

A tanker plane refuels a fighter jet over Iraq. Refueling in midair is a complicated process and even a slight error in judgment can result in tragedy.

long, 38 feet high, and has a wing span of almost 131 feet. It can fly 610 miles per hour while carrying over 31,000 gallons of gasoline, a load that weighs over 200,000 pounds.

Its crew consists of a pilot, copilot, and boom operator. As boom operator, it was Master Sergeant Marlin Mosley's task to connect a hose to a plane that needed fuel, called the receiver. Mosley explains how this is done:

> I'm basically guiding the receiver in with lights that are underneath the [tanker]. The pilot watches the lights, which I turn on and off to help guide the plane up into proper position. The lights tell the pilot to go up, down, or further to the side. I also talk to the pilot on the radio to help maneuver the plane into the right position so it can get fuel. When it is in the right spot, I lower the boom to their fuel receptor [an opening on the plane] and it automatically attaches itself so fuel can be delivered. It can be difficult and dangerous, especially when there are strong winds. [37]

The complicated process takes only a few minutes, but the entire experience can be nerve-racking for pilots. Navy commander John Geragotelis admitted he is always nervous when refueling because it involves flying close to other planes waiting to refuel, at speeds of up to three hundred miles per hour: "Rendezvousing on the tanker is usually the most dangerous part of the mission. There is high potential to collide with someone else, because lots of planes are arriving from different altitudes and directions." When the pilot met his tanker over Baghdad on the war's first day, he had to wait in line behind three other planes. When Geragotelis finally got his turn, he jokingly told the tanker crew, "Fill 'er up." [38]

Sea Power

When Geragotelis finished his mission, he flew back to an aircraft carrier like hundreds of other pilots. Even though there were no Iraqi ships to battle, the navy played a significant role in the war. For example, it helped secure the vital seaport of Umm Qasr, which allowed U.S. forces to more easily move war supplies into Iraq. However, the navy's greatest contribution to the Iraq War was launching planes and firing missiles from its ships.

The navy sent five aircraft carriers to the area. The *Kitty Hawk, Abraham Lincoln,* and *Constellation* were based in the Persian Gulf, while the *Harry Truman* and *Theodore Roosevelt* were in the Mediterranean Sea. By mid-April, the navy had already flown about half of the war's fifteen thousand air strikes and fired more than eight hundred missiles. That was a huge jump from the 1991 Gulf War, when navy fliers flew less than a quarter of all strike sorties and fired three hundred missiles.

The giant carriers were the key component of battle groups, which included a half-dozen or more other types of ships. These vessels included large ships designed to protect carriers from enemy ships; small minesweepers that locate and destroy mines that might be in the ocean; and submarines which fire missiles. What the vast majority of sailors on these ships had in common was that they all fought from long distance and lived far from their targets.

Life on Carriers

For sailors, serving on an aircraft carrier was like living in a floating city of steel and iron. The *Abraham Lincoln*, for example, which has a nuclear-powered engine, is almost eleven hundred feet long and weighs about ninety thousand tons. The ship's primary role is to serve as an airstrip for some one hundred planes. The huge, flat flight deck on which aircraft take off and land is the ship's most

Landing on an Aircraft Carrier

A night landing on an aircraft carrier is one of the most difficult tasks a jet pilot must master. Navy commander John Geragotelis says that when his plane first approaches the aircraft carrier, he is so high and far away that it seems "I'm looking at a postage stamp with blinking centerline lights." In an article he wrote for the *Journal of Electronic Defense,* Geragotelis explains how he made a landing on the USS *Constellation* after a mission over Baghdad on the first day of the Iraq War.

Now I'm too high and fast—better than low and slow, but still not pretty. I [cut back] some power until I see the ball [a visual indicator of where he is in relation to the ship on the instrument panel in front of him] starting to settle lower. Experience tells me I'm over the ramp. I add some power to break my descent. The jet touches down.

Landing on the deck of an aircraft carrier, particularly at night, is a very difficult task.

prominent feature. As long as three-and-a-half football fields and taking up 4.5 acres of space, the deck gives aircraft carriers their nickname "flat tops."

The flight deck, however, is only the most visible part of a huge ship that houses nearly five thousand men and women on voyages that can last many months. Below the main deck there are eighteen levels that have to be navigated by climbing up and down countless ladders and walking through seemingly endless narrow corridors. The ship contains hundreds of rooms and compartments that house sailors and aviators. These vast vessels even have their own post offices, television and radio stations, newspapers, libraries, hospitals, and small businesses such as a general store and barbershop.

Living and working in the bowels of such a huge ship can be strange. Because there are no windows, it is easy for people who stay below deck to lose track of whether it is night or day. "It's weird. The time, it just goes away from us. It's like we're at a standstill. It's like we're frozen for six months," is the way Airman Martin Rioja of the USS *Constellation* described the experience of a long voyage. Living on a large ship also means constantly being surrounded by steel walls and living and working in cramped rooms. "Everything's small. You just get used to it after a while,"[39] said sailor J. Dillon about the tiny size of most rooms.

Like their counterparts fighting on land, carrier personnel have to work long shifts to prepare for war or to wage it. During the air campaign, some sailors on the *Abraham Lin-*

coln put in twenty-hour shifts, assembling up to thirty bombs every two hours. The hard work was worth it for Sailor Mike Oglesbee, who took satisfaction from watching a television news show that highlighted destruction caused by bombs he had built. "I watched them go off in Baghdad," he said. "It felt so good to me to know that I had put those things together."[40]

Sailors and airmen on carriers were rewarded for their hard work with amenities ground troops could only dream about. One of the best perks was eating hot food prepared by good cooks. Chief Petty Officer George Porretta of the USS *Constellation* explains the mountain of supplies he needed to feed the crew:

> In my storeroom, I keep on hand almost $2 million worth of food. To give you a rough example of what we go through in a month, I utilize about 10,000 pounds of fresh potatoes, 7,000 pounds of fresh lettuce. I go through 3,500 pounds of butter. We get everything from milk, eggs, cheese, all the way up to lobster and candy bars. Right now, we're allowed $8.43 per day per man. We've got 5,000 sailors on board here, so you're looking at something around $40,000 a day we can figure out a menu with.[41]

It took a lot of hard work to turn the mountains of food into edible meals for the thousands of sailors aboard an aircraft carrier. But teams of navy cooks, who are renowned for their culinary skills, and other mess room helpers worked around the clock to provide tasty, nutritious meals to nourish the hard-working sailors.

In addition to better meals than ground troops had, men and women serving on a carrier also had more opportunities for recreation. They could watch movies or television, work out in a gym, enter a boxing tournament, and even play bingo for jackpots as high as $14,000.

Life on Other Ships

However, not every sailor liked carrier life. Many sailors preferred serving on a "small boy," the naval term for a ship smaller than a carrier. Indeed, life aboard smaller vessels is far different from life on the enormous carriers.

In many ways, life on a small ship is more like living in a town instead of a big city; there are so many sailors aboard big ships that a person is constantly running into strangers, which can make life less comfortable. Fireman Jesse Merrill of the small boy USS *Gary* experienced this when he had to go aboard the aircraft carrier *Kitty Hawk* to be treated for an injured knee. "It was almost traumatizing," he said. "By the third day, I was saying, 'Can I go back to my ship?'" The carrier had twenty-two times the *Gary*'s 250 sailors, and Merrill missed the close-knit friendships and camaraderie that comes from knowing almost everyone on a smaller vessel. The impersonal nature of serving on a larger ship was illustrated when Merrill was ordered by doctors to walk around the *Kitty Hawk* to exercise his knee. He became irri-

tated when sailors who did not recognize him thought he was goofing off because he was not working. Said Merrill, "I was asked six times in one day, 'Shouldn't you be at a cleaning station?'" [42]

Many of Merrill's shipmates agreed that they preferred smaller ships. For one thing, the *Gary* was low enough to the water to allow them to fish over its side, a favorite pastime. "It's a great stress-buster," admitted Kevin Pfeninger, who like other sailors enjoyed cooking and eating fish he caught. There are other types of fun on smaller ships, too. Several days each week on the *Gary* were designated for special morale-boosting activities. On Friday nights, for example, sailors took turns baking pizza for supper and on Saturday no one had to shave. Wednesday was a double treat—"Any Hat Day," in which sailors could wear bandannas or any other head gear, and "Siesta Wednesday," which allowed most to relax from 11 A.M. to 2 P.M. The break in routine "lets people recharge their batteries," [43] said Lieutenant Commander Mark Metzger, the ship's executive officer.

One type of ship, however, was less comfortable than both aircraft carriers and small boys—a submarine. Submarines are small and isolated; some are submerged for months at a time. Lieutenant Jason Perusek served on USS *Toledo*, a nuclear-powered sub that operated in the Red Sea firing missiles. He said of the sub's cramped quarters, "It's like living inside of a tank, with no place to hide." [44] He had to share a tiny room with two other officers, and their bunks were

The USS Toledo, *a nuclear-powered submarine, surfaces to take on supplies. The cramped quarters of the sub made life difficult for many sailors.*

stacked so close together that when he laid down to sleep, there was only four inches of clearance between his nose and the bunk above him. And water was at such a premium that sailors were allowed only a few seconds each day to shower.

The USS *Comfort*—a Hospital Ship

Of all the ships assembled for the Iraq War, perhaps the most unusual was the USS *Com-* *fort,* an oil supertanker that had been converted to a floating hospital. The ship was outfitted with eleven operating rooms, a frozen-blood bank, and the capacity to treat one thousand patients. Also on board were high-tech medical machines that enabled the *Comfort*'s sixty doctors to X-ray something as small as a blood vessel. The *Comfort* helped save countless lives by providing advanced medical care to wounded combatants (both Americans and wounded Iraqis).

The *Comfort* was able to provide finer care than smaller land-based military medical units. In fact, the technology aboard ship allowed the crew to give patients the same quality of care they could get at a major medical facility in the United States. During the Iraq War the ship's crew of 1,200 treated nearly 330 patients, most for combat injuries. That was the largest wartime role a hospital ship had played since the Vietnam War more than three decades earlier. Seaman Melissa A. Moore said working on the *Comfort* was the biggest challenge she had ever faced: "It was quite an experience. We took care of anything you can imagine that would exist in a war. I've never seen anything like it before, probably won't ever again."[45]

Patients were brought to the *Comfort*, which was anchored in the Persian Gulf, by helicopter and boat. When the injured arrived aboard ship, they were taken to a receiving area that had fifty beds. After being examined to assess what kind of care they needed, they were moved to one of the operating rooms; most needed surgery because only the most badly wounded were brought there.

Even when they were not flooded with patients to care for, crew members were busy nearly all the time. In addition to their medical duties, most people aboard ship also were responsible for operating the ship. An emergency medical technician, for example, might also be a cook, and even doctors and nurses were assigned jobs to keep the *Comfort* running.

A team of doctors onboard the USS Comfort, *an oil supertanker converted into a hospital, operates on a patient.*

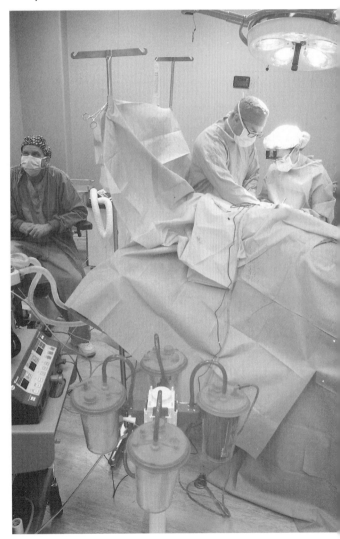

Going Home

After four months away from its home port of Baltimore, Maryland, and fifty-six days of active duty treating patients, the *Comfort* departed the Persian Gulf in early May with its mission completed. Although thousands of navy and air force personnel would remain in Iraq for months, many others were heading home—their part in the war had ended.

Many of the soldiers felt almost guilty that they could leave while others had to stay. Air Force Reserve captain Tim Martz, who had helped set up security measures at bases in Iraq, explained the complex emotions he felt upon returning home to Milwaukee in May 2003:

> You go through kind of a withdrawal period, where you miss it and you want to be there, basically for two reasons. One, because your brothers in arms are there. And two, because you get so involved in it and so committed to it, it's part of you and you start missing it. [46]

Chapter 3

Ground Troops in the Iraq War

Ground-level combat in which soldiers fight in close quarters, sometimes face-to-face, is one of the most powerful, horrifying experiences anyone will ever have to endure. The scenes of death and destruction, the sounds of bullets whizzing by, and the pungent smells of gunpowder and death assault soldiers' senses in an overpowering way, making combat difficult to comprehend even as it is happening.

After several weeks of fighting had carried the U.S. Army's Fourth Battalion, Sixty-fourth Armored Regiment north through Iraq from Kuwait to Baghdad, Specialist Royce Arcay struggled to come to terms with what he had experienced. Like many people, his conception of war had come from watching television shows or movies. But after living through it, Arcay admitted that war was far different than he imagined: "It sure didn't seem like what they put on TV. It's just kind of weird looking at dead bodies. They don't look real."[47]

For marine Michael Mead, the reality of war hit home hard when he was wounded in a battle in southern Iraq. While fighting with the First Battalion, Second Marine Regiment, his right leg was shredded by bits of metal after a rocket-propelled grenade struck the armored vehicle in which he was riding. "People at home don't get the real story of war. They don't see the blood and the pain. This isn't a game,"[48] Mead said from his hospital bed.

Although combat would be the war's defining experience for most ground troops, the men and women who battled their way over Iraq's highways and through its barren deserts discovered that there were many other challenges and hardships. One of the most formidable was the weather.

Sand, Mud, Heat

The Iraq desert proved to be an inhospitable environment for American soldiers. The first hardship was very hot weather; temperatures were in the 90s when the war began but

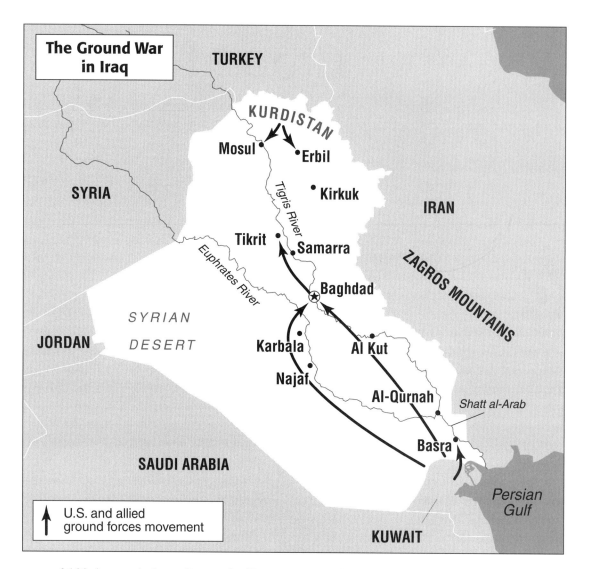

The Ground War in Iraq

topped 100 degrees in just a few weeks. Even worse were violent desert storms, which few Americans had ever experienced. When a powerful storm struck the advancing columns of U.S. troops on March 25, 2003, heavy winds, lack of visibility, and the stinging sand grains mercilessly battered soldiers, bringing the invasion to a temporary halt.

The storm made life miserable for soldiers. When the violent storm made marines take cover in southern Iraq, Lance Corporal Matthew Hatcher could only wonder aloud, "Where does the wind come from? Where does it come from? It just doesn't stop," while Sergeant Rod Richard commented, "I think this is like right out of a science fiction movie."[49] Tons of swirling sand covered sleeping soldiers with a thick blanket of grit and fouled the mechanisms of their guns, forcing them to clean their weapons continuously. Blowing sand also dirtied their food before they could eat it and made breathing difficult.

Even when soldiers tried to protect themselves by wrapping cloth around their faces, tiny sand grains blasted their way into their eyes, noses, ears, and mouths. Said marine Jerry Collins, "You never felt clean. You always felt like you'd just spent the day at the beach, gritty and dirty."[50]

Intense rains also made life difficult for soldiers traversing Iraq. Near the end of March 2003, for example, it rained steadily for days, making it difficult for paratroopers parachuting into an airfield to land. The ground was so mushy that the army and air force paratroopers, loaded down with heavy weapons and other supplies, sank into the mire and had to struggle to make it to harder, drier ground.

Soldiers also sweltered in desert temperatures that during the day neared 120 degrees. Adding to the discomfort were protective suits soldiers had to wear because of the threat of attacks with chemicals such as nerve gas or germs. The hot temperatures and the chemical suits made soldiers sweat profusely. To prevent them from becoming dehydrated, soldiers had to drink lots of liquids, consuming up to several gallons a day. The heat was so bad it made it difficult just to sleep, especially for soldiers who had to get their rest during the day. But adequate sleep was just one of many things soldiers had to do without during combat.

The Road to Baghdad

The infantry units that fought their way through Iraq in the first weeks of the war had to do without ordinary things that most people take for granted—water to wash with, a bed to sleep in, and decent food. Although the military normally provides soldiers tasty, nourishing meals, in the field they eat MREs, the prepackaged military meals. Many soldiers did not like MREs very much because they were not very tasty. The MREs, however, came with packets of hot sauce, and most soldiers liberally doused it on whatever they ate to cover up the taste. After weeks or even months of eating MREs, some soldiers said they had become hooked on hot sauce and poured it on everything they ate.

Sometimes during combat, even MREs were scarce. During the push to Baghdad, for example, supply lines extending back to Kuwait became disrupted. Because of this, soldiers were sometimes limited to one MRE a day, had to scavenge for anything edible they could find, or even went hungry. In a diary entry dated March 26, 2003, marine Joseph Nasrallah wrote that while fighting in the town of Nasiriyah, "All [we] had to eat was bread and onions."[51]

A lack of food was not the only hardship for soldiers making their way north to Baghdad. The trip was a tough one even though most were able to ride in tanks, armored vehicles, and trucks that traveled in large groups for safety. At night when the convoys stopped, most soldiers slept in sleeping bags in the open desert; a lucky few were able to find shelter in vehicles. There was water to drink but none for bathing, which meant they could not wash away the coarse sand that found its way into every inch of their clothing. As a result, their clothes became dirty and smelly.

In the first week of March near the city of Karbala, Sergeant Bill Endsley was amazed at how being denied such basic necessities had affected his fellow soldiers. Said Endsley:

Combat Conditions

Mark Oliva is a gunnery sergeant in the marines as well as a reporter for the military newspaper *Stars and Stripes.* In one of his stories, titled "Iraq War: Making History, Making Marines," Oliva wrote about the difficult experiences of combat. Oliva described the horror of seeing dead enemy soldiers: "Bodies of dead Iraqis, twisted, torn in half and mangled, littered the roads. The sickening, sweet smell of burned flesh lingers in the nostrils for days." He also wrote about some of the physical discomfort soldiers endured, like having to wear dirty clothes for days, not being able to wash properly, and having the skin on their hands become so dry from the desert heat and winds that it cracked and bled. Oliva also explained that in combat situations, there was often not enough food to eat or water to drink because it was hard to keep soldiers supplied with them: "Even chows [meals] are cut to one a day for a while and water is as precious as bullets. Wedding rings get strapped to watchbands because they no longer stay on the fingers. They've lost too much weight."

When the soldiers first leave home, it's about all the things they want most when they're at home [friends, social activities, their favorite foods]. Then, when they've been here a while, it's about a shower, or a bed, or wondering what it's like not to wear the same uniform for a month.[52]

Camp Life

Living conditions for soldiers improved when they were able to make temporary or permanent camps. Often, the soldiers had to create them out of rugged terrain that at first glance looked unlivable. In early April when marine Mike Koole viewed the barren spot in the Iraq desert where his marine unit was supposed to make a base to distribute fuel to military vehicles, he could not believe it: "We looked around and said, 'No way!' There was nothing here—no trees, no grass, nothing."[53]

But with a lot of work, the camp soon took form as a city of tents quickly sprouted in the desert. The different-sized tents provided places to sleep, eat, and work—and some tents were even air conditioned. Soldiers were also able to clean off desert sand and grime in crude showers made by hanging plastic water bags in plywood stalls, with a water nozzle inserted at the top.

Once a camp had been established and soldiers were in one place for more than a few hours, mail caught up with them. Receiving packages from home loaded with treats greatly boosted soldiers' spirits. Some

Many camps had crude showers like this one, which were made by hanging a plastic water container in a plywood stall.

camps also had telephones, which soldiers could use to call loved ones. Almost as important to morale were improved sanitary facilities. Instead of shallow trenches dug in the sand or simply the nearest bush, soldiers had

more comfort and privacy—even toilet paper. Inhabitants of a marine camp in central Iraq were delighted with makeshift bathrooms that, by the standards of wartime Iraq, were fancy—they had wooden seats and camouflage netting for privacy. "We're pretty spoiled here,"[54] admitted Navy officer Kathryn Fauss.

Soldiers in combat rarely enjoyed such amenities. However, while they were fighting during the period of major combat, they were more worried about staying alive than having such creature comforts.

Combat

As American soldiers made their way through Iraq, the giant battles that many had envisioned being involved in never occurred. Because the Iraqi army of 1 million men never made a decisive stand to stop the invading force, most of the fighting consisted of short, quick encounters between relatively small groups of combatants.

In the first few weeks of the Iraq War, U.S. soldiers discovered how suddenly combat could occur. A few days after the fighting began, marine Joseph Willems was walking toward a bunker that Iraqi soldiers had dug in the sand when he saw the muzzle blast from a rifle. "I looked down and saw shots being fired, and I just went 'ooooh,' and jumped back," said Willems. "[I] saw a guy in a blue sweatshirt, and took a hip shot with my saw [machine gun]."[55] Willems killed the enemy soldier.

For most American soldiers, the Iraq War was the first time they had experienced combat. When it was thrust upon them, they had to quickly call up the training they had received on how to deal with combat situations. That was the way it happened for soldiers Brian Saladin and Richard Bear when their Humvees were attacked while crossing a bridge over the Euphrates River. "We did what we were supposed to," said Saladin. "We all faced out, said, 'This is my [area to defend],' and started shooting." Bear said the battle was a blur; it happened so quickly he did not realize what was actually going on. Bear recalled, "I didn't have time to think about my wife, my kids, my cat, my dogs. It's not until afterward when you say, 'Wow, we were getting shot at and blown up.'"[56]

The majority of combat situations were quick encounters that occurred when Iraqi soldiers attacked U.S. convoys heading north to Baghdad or when American soldiers entered and took control of cities. These brief clashes erupted quickly and were intense. This type of fight broke out as marines approached Diwaniyah, a community about eighty miles southeast of Baghdad. Iraqi soldiers were hiding in a series of trenches and also concealed in buildings and behind vehicles. When the shooting started, it was confusing for Americans because the enemy seemed to be everywhere. "They [Iraqi soldiers] just exploded out of the buildings, out of [nearby] trees, everywhere,"[57] said Captain Brian Lewis.

The firefight (the military term for an armed encounter with the enemy) lasted forty-five minutes and eventually became centered on a heavily fortified military post

Comrades in Arms

When soldiers go into combat, deep bonds of trust and friendship develop between individual soldiers. In September 2003, the Strategic Studies Institute at the U.S. Army War College published a study titled "Why They Fight: Combat Motivation in the Iraq War." It was based on interviews with soldiers who fought in the war. According to the study, when soldiers were asked "What was most important to you [during combat] in making you want to keep going and do as well as you could?", the most common response was "Fighting for my buddies." The following are excerpts from the study.

One soldier simply stated, "I know that as far as myself, sir, I take my squad mates' lives more important than my own." Another soldier related the intense burden he felt for his fellow soldiers, "That person means more to you than anybody. You will die if he dies. That is why I think that we protect each other in any situation. I know that if he dies and it was my fault, it would be worse than death to me." . . . One soldier stated, "It is just like a big family. Nothing can come to you without going through them first. It is kind of comforting." One soldier attempted to describe . . . the close relationship he had with another soldier . . . "I knew Taylor would personally look out for me. . . . It was stupid little things like, 'Dude, you look like you need a hug.' He would come over and give me a big old bear hug. He knew that I looked out for him and vice versa. . . . I trusted Taylor was going to keep an eye on everything. He always did. Obviously, he did. We are still here. Thank God."

in a grove of palm trees. U.S. forces eventually drove off the Iraqis with cannons able to fire shells from miles away. Superior weapons enabled U.S. soldiers to often win these armed engagements in a short time. Some confrontations, however, lasted longer.

Bigger Battles

One of the most prolonged battles occurred at Nasiriyah, which was one of the most hotly contested strategic points on the highway to Baghdad. At Nasiriyah, U.S. troops had to make their way over two bridges spanning the Euphrates River. The battle over the beleaguered stretch of road lasted several days and Iraqis kept striking at different spots. Sergeant Chris Merkle called the battle a "turkey shoot" because it reminded him of old-fashioned shooting contests in which marksmen shot turkeys tethered to one spot. The soldiers, Merkle meant, were as vulnerable as such birds. "Each unit," said Merkle, "takes its turn being sacrificed. Everybody gets torn apart the same way."[58]

Nevertheless, the U.S. forces had to keep traveling the dangerous stretch of road because their job was to move supplies along the highway to soldiers farther north. As the trucks rolled through, Iraqis dug in along the road attacked with rifles, machine guns, and rocket-propelled grenades. In just one day the Iraqis destroyed seven large trucks and wounded sixty marines. It took U.S. forces nearly a week to finally secure the stretch of road.

One of the fiercest battles was over Saddam International Airport in Baghdad. The First Brigade Combat Team began its assault on April 2, 2003, following a two-day bombardment by air force planes and army rockets and artillery to weaken the Iraqi army. The drive to take the airport began at night under cover of darkness, which soldier Ernest Marcone explained is a dangerous time to fight because it is hard to see the enemy: "When we got through the walls, there was no illumination and we had no idea where the enemy [was. Fighting at night is] probably the most difficult mission a task force can undertake."[59] After three hours of vicious fighting, U.S. forces prevailed. During the battle, they killed some 250 Iraqi soldiers. They also destroyed or captured forty tanks as well as many artillery pieces and antiaircraft guns.

Reaction to Combat

Although most combat was not as dramatic as the battle to take the airport, many soldiers were involved in heavy fighting in the early weeks of the war. Some soldiers found combat exhilarating because they were finally able to use the combat skills they had worked to acquire. "I'm in my happy place,"[60] is the way Marine lieutenant colonel Bryan P. McCoy put it in April while leading his men into battle in Diwaniyah.

But for many others the reality of combat, especially killing the enemy, overwhelmed them emotionally. Even a veteran like thirty-five-year-old soldier Thomas Slago, who had been in the army since he was a teenager, had trouble coping with his feelings. "I didn't think it would be like this, killing people,"[61] Slago said after killing at least five enemy soldiers. Also troubled by his combat experience was Martin Vera, who reenlisted in the marines after the September 11, 2001, terrorist attacks because he wanted to defend his country. In March, Vera was upset after shooting at Iraqi soldiers after a battle at an oil pumping station in southern Iraq. Said Vera, "After 9-11 it was like, yeah, I wanted to [fight]. But it bothered me, shooting at those guys. I had to do it; it's my job. But it bothered me. A lot."[62]

For some soldiers, their reaction was so severe that they began having nightmares or feelings of anxiety, depression, and guilt about what they had done or experienced. Soldiers spoke with chaplains or doctors to overcome such psychological problems, which are referred to as posttraumatic stress. For most soldiers, that was enough to help them deal with their emotions. Some combatants, however, had to be sent home to U.S. military hospitals for further treatment.

This psychological anguish was just one type of scar from combat. Many soldiers suffered a wide variety of physical wounds, and some were killed. Although Iraqis had less equipment and training than the U.S. soldiers they faced, they often fought bravely and effectively. And that translated into U.S. casualties—the military term for a soldier who is wounded, killed, or reported missing in action.

Wounded and Killed

The scariest thing about combat is that a soldier can be killed or wounded at any time. Like many others, soldier Dave Jotich discovered in early April how quickly and unexpectedly this could occur when he was wounded by a land mine that exploded while he was walking near Baghdad. Said Jotich, "I didn't really hear it. It was kind of like a bang, and he [a soldier with him] was already down. I turned around and walked in a circle. I looked down at my leg, and it was bloody."[63]

But when U.S. soldiers were wounded, they received the best care ever given in combat. They were first treated in the field by medics trained to deal with combat wounds. They were then evacuated from the combat zone to nearby hospitals, including the USS *Comfort,* a floating hospital in the Persian Gulf with beds for one thousand patients. More seriously wounded soldiers were flown to the U.S. military's Landstuhl Regional Medical Center in Germany. Jotich, for example, was taken to the 212th Mobile Army Surgical Hospital (MASH), a medical unit that travels into combat zones. The 212th MASH also treated captured Iraqi soldiers and civilians such as a seven-year-old boy who had been wounded by a tank.

Even with the best medical treatment available, some soldiers succumb to their injuries and die. Between March 20 and May 1, 2003, when President George W. Bush declared major combat had ended, 138 U.S. soldiers were killed (and hundreds more were killed in the year-long period after that). Although it can be difficult to deal with the death of a friend, in combat soldiers have to learn to ignore their emotions

A marine helps a wounded comrade to safety. Soldiers wounded in battle were treated by medics specially trained to work in combat situations.

when that happens. Lieutenant Colonel Ernest "Rock" Marcone explains why: "Whatever emotions you're feeling, you've got to take the pain, let your instincts take over. You've got to concentrate on the guys who are alive. They [the dead] are just bodies. Their spirits are gone."[64]

Marcone's advice may sound brutal, but it was realistic. Grieving for dead comrades could take their minds off the task at hand and get other soldiers killed. But there was

one type of death for which that advice was especially difficult to practice—soldiers accidentally killed by their own side.

Friendly Fire

During the heat of battle, soldiers sometimes accidentally kill their own comrades.

Such a death is said to have been due to "friendly fire" and the circumstances surrounding it are considered to have occurred in the "fog of war," the confusion and chaos that often surrounds combat. During the 1991 Persian Gulf War, thirty-five U.S. soldiers were killed in friendly fire incidents. Although the military worked to limit such incidents, several occurred again in the 2003 Iraq War. Typical of such incidents in which soldiers on the same side may wind up mistakenly fighting each other was a firefight near Nasiriyah. In his diary entry after the battle, marine Joseph Nasrallah wrote, "We got in a firefight with Iraqi soldiers and friendly Marines. We didn't know who each other was."[65]

Although he will never know for sure, Nasrallah may have been wounded by a fellow American soldier. But it was definitely friendly fire that killed Army captain Ed Korn in a battle about fifteen miles southeast of Baghdad. When Korn strayed into enemy lines near an Iraqi tank that had just been destroyed, he was mistaken for an Iraqi soldier. Major Kent Rideout gave the order to shoot what he and other soldiers thought was an Iraqi soldier about to attack. When Rideout realized what had happened, he was devastated. But he still believes he acted correctly: "I've replayed it over in my mind a hundred times, and I still would do it the same way. [However,] this was the worst day of my Army career. No doubt, the worst day. I get to go home with that. I get to live with that the rest of my life."[66]

It was another kind of mistake, a fatal wrong turn for a convoy of army trucks, that led some American soldiers to become prisoners of war (POWs).

POWs in the Iraq War

In combat situations, even a small error can lead to a major disaster. That is what happened on March 23, 2003, when a convoy of eighteen trucks from the army's 507th Maintenance Company made a wrong turn near Nasiriyah. Instead of bypassing the Iraqi stronghold, which they were supposed to do, the soldiers driving the trucks mistakenly headed into town and were attacked. In the ensuing fight seventeen soldiers were killed and seven were captured, including Private Jessica Lynch, who became the most famous POW of the Iraq War.

The soldiers on the trucks were support personnel such as cooks, supply clerks, and mechanics, and thus had not been trained as frontline infantry soldiers. Regardless, they put up a spirited fight for an hour and a half before realizing they had no choice but to surrender or be killed. Soldier Patrick Miller compared their position to that of General George Armstrong Custer, who along with more than two hundred of his men died in the Battle of the Little Bighorn in 1876:

We were like Custer. We were surrounded. We had no working weapons [sand and dirt jammed their rifles]. We couldn't even make a bayonet charge—we would have been mowed down. We didn't have a choice.[67]

The survivors were beaten with sticks, kicked, and held prisoner. Although Lynch was taken to a hospital in Nasiriyah, the others were moved around constantly. The POWs were questioned but not tortured. However, the Iraqis violated international standards on POW treatment by televising scenes of the bodies of soldiers who died in the ambush. They also showed footage of the survivors being interrogated. Although Miller said it was "degrading" to be filmed, he admitted he felt relieved when it happened. "They were putting us on TV," he said, "so I knew they wouldn't do anything to us."[68]

Saving Private Lynch

In a daring raid on the night of April 1, 2003, soldiers rescued Private Jessica Lynch from a hospital in Nasiriyah where she was being held as a prisoner of war. The following account of her rescue is from *I Am a Soldier, Too: The Jessica Lynch Story,* by Rick Bragg.

[Lynch heard voices asking "Where is Jessica Lynch?"] Inside her room, Jessi cowered under her covers. What if it was Saddam's people, come to get her again? It didn't matter that the words were English; so many Iraqis spoke English. "Oh, God," Jessi thought, "don't let it be them." She could not see the door clearly because of the curtain. She lay, her good hand clutching the sheet to her chin, and refused to answer. There was some light in the room, enough to see a man's form as he walked in. And then, just like she had wished it, a soldier was standing there by her bed. He took off his helmet so she could see him better. "Jessica Lynch," he said, "we're United States soldiers, and we're here to protect you and take you home." [She answered,] "I'm an American soldier, too." The soldier reached to his shoulder and ripped a patch from his uniform and pressed it into her free hand. "And I held on to that patch and held on to his hand, and I was afraid to let go." They laid her gently but quickly on a stretcher and carried her down the hall and into the stairwell. They passed quickly into the courtyard, and Jessi felt the wind from the rotors wash over her. Someone was still holding her hand. The helicopter lifted off, its rotor blades slicing through the dark. "O.K., this is real. This is real," thought Jessi. "I'm going home."

Private Jessica Lynch was rescued in a daring night mission on April 1, 2003.

The POWs were finally freed on April 13, 2003, when marines rescued them from a home on the outskirts of Tikrit. Specialist Shoshana Johnson, who was wounded by bullets in both feet while fighting the Iraqis, said that at first the marines did not recognize the prisoners of war as Americans because they were dressed in striped pajamas that the Iraqis had made them wear. "They said, 'Get down, get down,' and one of them said, 'No, she's American.' I broke down. I was like, 'Oh, my God, I'm going home,'"[69] said Johnson, who was relieved she would live to see her three-year-old daughter, Janelle. Lynch was rescued separately on April 1 from a hospital in Nasiriyah.

A Real War

Major combat in the Iraq War lasted only six weeks. But for those who lived through that dangerous, harrowing period, they were some of the most memorable days of their lives. As one soldier, Leo Montiel, put it:

> This was a real war—with fronts, ambushes, patrols, house-to-house combat. We earned the ground we gained. It was not just an air war. You actually saw the enemy. It was personal. There were real casualties. But everyone that I met . . . who had been wounded said they had no regrets.[70]

Chapter 4

U.S. Soldiers Help Rebuild Iraq

When major combat in the Iraq War ended, Iraqi teacher Keloid Rheem returned to her classroom in the village of Shanafiya where she had once taught young girls. The Iraqi teacher found that all the windows had been broken and looters had stolen everything they could, including light and fan fixtures. This did not matter much, however, because there was no electricity to run them. "Only picture. All gone," Rheem said sadly, noting that all that remained on the walls of the barren room were a few science posters. Her words were directed to soldier Rich Appel. His job was to examine hundreds of similarly gutted classrooms in the province of Al Qadisiyah and figure out how to restore and equip them so children could return to school. "There's so many needs it's overwhelming," Appel admitted. [71]

Reopening schools was just one part of the monumental job that confronted U.S. soldiers when major combat operations in Iraq ended. Although private companies performed much of the major reconstruction work in the war-torn nation, the military helped repair schools, hospitals, and other public buildings. They also helped build highways, bridges, and airports. Some soldiers worked to reestablish the nation's shattered economy, while others restored utilities such as electricity and water. The military also helped create local police forces and other agencies so Iraqis could prepare to govern themselves.

Rebuilding Iraq was a huge task. In fact, it was the U.S. military's biggest, most complex reconstruction project since the end of World War II, when America had helped rebuild Japan and Germany after defeating them. Although the work was difficult and often frustrating, many soldiers enjoyed it because they felt they were helping people. As one soldier put it, "Every day you go out, you touch lives. You do good—it's a huge warm and fuzzy [feeling]." [72]

Help in the Midst of War

Even while Iraq was still engulfed in war in March and April 2003, U.S. soldiers were giving Iraqi citizens food and water so they could survive. Some soldiers, such as marine Dave Long, passed out bags of candy to hungry Iraqi kids. Soldiers also passed out more substantial fare, including their own prepackaged MREs.

Many American soldiers were touched by the poverty-stricken, hungry people that greeted them as they advanced through Iraq. Marine Joshua Smith said he had been dismayed to see barefoot children selling Iraqi cigarettes to soldiers—this was one of

An Iraqi girl carries away bottled water and food given to her by U.S. soldiers.

the only ways they could get money to buy food. "You see something like that on the [television] commercials where you can adopt a kid [sponsor a child from another country]. That stuff just doesn't happen in the States,"[73] Smith said.

U.S. soldiers also brought tons of supplies into Iraq to feed people suffering from the war's destruction. With markets and stores closed, Iraqis had to depend on food the soldiers brought into their areas on trucks and other vehicles. An equally serious problem in many areas was a lack of water. Military trucks thus hauled bottled water to towns throughout Iraq. Soldiers sometimes even rebuilt pipelines to deliver water. A rebuilt pipeline to Umm Qasr, for example, provided the area's residents with 400,000 gallons of drinkable water a day.

Another important commodity the military sometimes helped provide was gasoline. This resource was scarce because Saddam Hussein's regime had confiscated fuel reserves for the war. Citizens needed gasoline to run trucks, tractors, cars, and generators that produced electricity. Soldiers played a role in securing gasoline for Iraqis. For example, near the town of Al Kut, marines discovered a fuel trailer that Iraqi soldiers had abandoned after it became stuck in mud. After several hours of backbreaking work to free the vehicle, they distributed the fuel to residents of Sbah, a small nearby village. Sergeant Matthew E. Schettler, who speaks Arabic, said village leader Abu Jasam told him the fuel "is a great blessing." Schettler predicted villagers will fondly remember the

charitable act for a long time: "This free fuel was a real find, something they'll tell their grandchildren about."[74]

Another way soldiers helped Iraqis was to protect civilians so they would not be injured or killed during combat. As American troops advanced into Iraq, they encountered many people, sometimes entire families, who were fleeing from their homes because they feared they would be killed during a battle between U.S. and Iraqi forces. American soldiers helped create camps where these refugees could live temporarily until the fighting ended and they could return to their homes. U.S. soldiers also gave the refugees medical care for injuries or illness. Iraqi soldiers and civilians, in fact, were often treated in the same military hospitals in which U.S. soldiers were cared for. The military also set up small clinics in some areas specifically for civilians.

A New Mission

After American soldiers defeated Iraqi forces, they were called on to perform many tasks to help Iraqis begin rebuilding their nation. Although much of the job of rebuilding postwar Iraq was done by soldiers in civil affairs units who had special training in such tasks, every soldier helped the country recover in some way.

The biggest initial job facing U.S. soldiers when combat ended was to provide security. The war had led to the collapse of the Iraqi government—this meant there were no longer any officials or government agencies to regulate vital services for civilians, such as police. Providing security was very difficult because many people used the postwar chaos to loot banks, government offices, museums, and other buildings. They took anything of value, including works of art and other relics of Iraq's past that were thousands of years old. For many months, U.S. forces patrolled cities as police to keep people safe from criminals.

Soldiers also continued to provide humanitarian aid in the form of food, water, and medical care. While doing this, they began assessing how to rebuild roads, bridges, electric plants, schools, and other buildings that had been destroyed or damaged by the war.

However, in the first few weeks after major combat ended, it was hard for U.S. soldiers to make the switch from fighting and defending themselves against an enemy army to helping people in need. They had just spent six weeks fighting and killing Iraqi soldiers, and now they were expected to undertake a peacekeeping mission. For many soldiers, the new duties they were assigned in the postwar period created "mission confusion," a term used to describe the psychological shift they had to make. Army lieutenant Will Riley explained the problem as "a very difficult transition. We have a mission one minute to go out and kill it if it moves— and then suddenly we have to protect and police [civilians]."[75]

Many soldiers found it difficult to shake themselves out of the warring mentality they had developed during combat. Soldier Robert Blake explained that to do their new jobs, soldiers had to change the way they thought about people they encountered: "Just coming out of combat it sounds like a crazy thing to tell someone, but I found myself telling [other soldiers]: 'Relax, dude— everybody is not out to kill you.'"[76]

Although making that mental switch and assuming new responsibilities was often difficult for soldiers, their superior officers knew it was vital that they do it. Now that Saddam Hussein had been overthrown, U.S. soldiers had to help rebuild Iraq so its citizens could start their lives over again.

Teaching Democracy

Saddam had brutally ruled Iraq for over three decades. A dictator who wielded ultimate power over his country, Saddam and his regime had denied Iraqis many rights that people who live in a democracy such as the United States take for granted. Citizens who criticized the government or angered Saddam or other officials in any way could be arrested and kept in jail for years without being formally charged or tried in a court. Sometimes they were kidnapped and executed.

Although there were elections, only candidates of the Baath Party, which Saddam controlled, could run for office, which meant that voters really had no choice in the officials they elected. Saddam and other party officials also strictly controlled the nation's economy and corruptly used this money to build hundreds of lavish palaces for themselves. Because of such corruption, there were limited government funds to

A Seabee's Account

The Seabees are the navy's construction force, sailors with a variety of skills who build things. In Iraq the Seabees erected buildings for U.S. personnel as well as schools and other structures. In a series of e-mails to American Legion Post 45 titled "The Straight Scoop: A Seabee's Firsthand Account of Life in Iraq," Senior Chief Art Messer talked about some improvements he witnessed.

The towns I saw a month ago with raw sewage running in the streets and between the buildings are now showing marked signs of improvement! I went through some towns a few days ago and the sewage was drained away and drying up. I saw new construction and building upgrades everywhere! I saw power lines being repaired and new utility lines being installed everywhere. I saw many Iraqis working and living and getting back to a normal life.... In the city of Hillah, the power stays on 24 hours a day and it has more power than prior to the war.... The Seabees have rebuilt all of the schools and put in furniture and chalkboards. The kids used to sit on the floor! Now they have nice desks to sit at. Commerce is running.... Life is flowing back in to this country and ... I am so glad I got to watch it happen. Some days watching the Iraqi people is like watching the faces of little kids on Christmas Day! Many of them are walking around in a daze wondering what to do with their freedom.

A group of Seabees, the navy's construction force, rebuilds a bridge near Zubaydiyah.

provide schools, health care, and other benefits for citizens.

After Saddam was overthrown, the major U.S. goal was to install democratic institutions in Iraq. The challenge in doing so often seemed overwhelming. For example, American troops sometimes helped arrange city council elections for municipalities of as many as a million residents. Soldiers helped local residents select candidates to run for office, register people to vote, and run the balloting. One American who helped in this process, Army lieutenant colonel Mark Garrell, noted that a free election had been a foreign concept to the Iraqis he worked with: "They're scared and they don't really know how democracy works. But for the first time [in decades] they have an assembly elected through a democratic process."[77]

Indeed, Iraqis had lived for so long in a corrupt and controlling society that they had to adjust to having personal freedom. One soldier shared his surprise that even after Saddam's regime had been overthrown, Iraqis still had trouble taking independent action because they feared they would be punished if they did the wrong thing:

> They wanted permission to do anything. One man wanted to get a part for his well pump, but he wouldn't go without a note from me. He was afraid if he was stopped, the police would think he stole the part. [Similarly,] teachers were afraid to teach without permission.[78]

A soldier hands a young girl a bag of school supplies. Children from Tampa, Florida, donated the supplies.

Rebuilding Schools

Soldiers also had a hand in repairing hundreds of schools in Iraq that had been damaged in the war. They also helped build scores of new ones. For example, in the Ninevah Province in northern Iraq, the 101st Airborne Division helped rebuild more than eight hundred schools. The construction cost over $2 million, a sum that was paid for with military funding meant expressly for rebuilding.

Many military personnel who helped work on the schools greatly enjoyed their work. One of them was Navy reservist Paul Hartje, who in 2003 helped rebuild five schools in the Diwaniyah area. He said he loved the job:

It was a great feeling. I have pictures of kids hugging us. And you could actually see more children coming to school from day to day as they realized Saddam was really out of power. The schools became flooded with kids. Just seeing their faces, they were so happy. That was a big reward for me.[79]

October 1, 2003, was an important date for children across Iraq: It was the first day of school for all public primary and secondary school students. In addition to attending classes in schools that had been built or repaired by the military, students also had access to books, pens, paper, and other school supplies which soldiers helped to donate. For example, members of the 422nd Civil Affairs Battalion asked friends and family members back home to send such supplies so they could give them to students at the Shahaba School in Baghdad.

The education children were receiving would equip them to do many different types of jobs when they grew up. And the U.S. military was already hard at work restoring Iraq's economy so that good jobs would be waiting for them in the future.

Economic Rebuilding

When the fighting ended, Iraq's economy was in shambles. Even before the war, the Iraqi economy had been weakened by sanctions the United Nations imposed on Iraq as a punishment for invading Kuwait in 1991. The UN sanctions limited the amount of oil Iraq could sell, which cut its main source of income. The country's economy had also been weakened by decades of corrupt and inefficient managing of its resources by its own officials. The fall of Saddam's regime and the devastation of the war further crippled the nation's economy and created widespread financial hardships for millions of Iraqis.

One problem was that people who depended on the government for salaries, pensions, or other benefits were left without any money. Even as the war continued in April 2003, military officials were sorting through records to figure out which citizens were entitled to funds from the former Iraqi regime. In June, when the 432nd Civil Affairs Battalion finally paid such funds to thirty thousand people in the Al Qadisiyah Province, Major John Hope said they were so anxious to get money that they created a mob scene.

Soccer Balls

In July 2003, members of the 352nd Civil Affairs Command delivered twelve hundred soccer balls and other athletic gear to youth centers in northern Iraq. Like children all over the world, boys and girls in Iraq love sports. One of the soldiers making the delivery was Sergeant Janis Albuquerque. In an army news release by Chad D. Wilkerson titled "U.S. Army Delivers Soccer Balls to Northern Iraq," Albuquerque explains why athletic equipment was important for Iraqi kids.

We dropped off the shipments and both the children and adults who were there were ecstatic. The donation of soccer balls and sports equipment was intended as a signal to the Kurds [the ethnic group that lives in northern Iraq] that we are genuinely interested in their future. Wherever the equipment ends up, I know that it will enhance the programs that are in place there and the youth will be able to enjoy it. With this new equipment, growth [in sports and recreation programs] is going to happen. More programs can be started and more youth will be able to participate.

"It was a zoo. People pushing, shoving, kicking, biting. It was an absolute near-riot every day." Sergeant Lahela Corrigan, however, said soldiers were gratified they were able to help distribute the funds because they knew the Iraqis desperately needed the money. "They're thrilled when they get paid. We're pumping money into the local economy. People are able to buy goods," she said.[80]

The money the military helped distribute began to ease the financial problems of those receiving it and helped strengthen Iraq's economy. In 2003, U.S. soldiers who had expertise in financial matters helped Iraqis create and put new currency into circulation. The old Iraqi bills, which featured Saddam's picture, were a scary reminder of his brutal regime and had to be replaced. Soldiers also helped the country begin pumping, refining, and selling oil, the country's most valuable resource. Indeed, oil sales would yield billions of dollars to help Iraq re-

cover from decades of neglect. The military helped Iraqis restart oil wells that were shut down before the war. They also helped repair damaged pipelines that carried oil to refineries, where it could be made into gasoline to be sold.

Although oil was Iraq's premier industry, the nation's economy needed many smaller businesses to provide goods and services people needed. Military units in various communities distributed funds earmarked for reconstruction to Iraqis so they could start new businesses. Army Lieutenant Anthony Coulter is an example of an American soldier who helped Iraqis revitalize their shattered economy. Coulter organized seminars to teach Iraqis how to launch new businesses. He also helped local leaders bring a commercial airline to Kirkuk, a city of 1 million people. The arrival of the airline would create jobs and help the local economy grow by bringing in travelers who would spend money. For Coulter, the Iraq War had brought an unexpected chance to practice what he had learned in college before joining the military. Said Coulter, "It's pretty wild. Only in a place like this, would a 24-year-old get to do what I'm doing. I never thought I'd use my business degree. It's a crazy world."[81]

The businesses that the military helped start in turn provided jobs for unemployed Iraqis, which was a key postwar task. Indeed, getting Iraqi men and women employed was critical to strengthening the country's emerging economy. To make it easier to find jobs in Iraq's capital city, an army unit in July opened the Baghdad Business Center, which became a place where workers and prospective employers could contact each other.

Police and Security Forces

While helping men and women find jobs was challenging for U.S. soldiers, filling one type of position was one of the most difficult and

Members of the new Iraqi Civil Defense Corps receive rifles from U.S. soldiers.

frustrating tasks of the postwar period—recruiting people to serve in the new Iraqi police and security forces. Although there had been enough U.S. and coalition soldiers to win the Iraq War, there were not enough of them to police and protect all 25 million Iraqis in the conflict's violent aftermath. The U.S. military thus began creating local police forces as well as a national Iraqi Civil Defense Corps, which would replace the country's defeated army.

It was difficult, however, to find eligible men and women to serve in these agencies. The easiest way to build a police force would have been to rehire all the people who had previously worked in law enforcement. But in Iraq, many of those who had once worked for police forces had been members of Saddam's Baath Party. They had treated prisoners brutally and even tortured them to obtain confessions. Although some former policemen were rehired, the U.S. military had to exclude many of them from serving on the new police units because of the way they had acted in the past.

Another huge challenge U.S. soldiers faced was training the new police recruits. The U.S. military wanted to modernize Iraqi police forces so they could do a better job of catching criminals and protecting citizens. This meant that even former police officers allowed to join the new units had to learn many new skills. The U.S. soldiers chosen for this job, most of whom had received either civilian or military law enforcement training, taught recruits new ways to investigate crimes, collect evidence, and interrogate prisoners.

They also showed the trainees the basics, such as how to use the pistols they were issued.

The hardest part of the training was to educate recruits to respect the rights of prisoners, something police under Saddam's rule had never done. Although a small number of U.S. troops were themselves later found to have abused captives under their watch, the training the Iraqi recruits received emphasized the humane treatment of prisoners. Captain Scott Southworth was one of the soldiers helping train a new police force. He said it was difficult to make police recruits understand that they had to treat prisoners humanely: "The transition from dictatorship to democracy takes time. We have to tell them that beating a suspect to get him to talk is not OK. They were like, 'We have to beat prisoners. How else will we get their confessions?'"[82]

Americans and Iraqis

In trying to build new security forces, U.S. soldiers came up against something that caused them problems in every phase of their effort to rebuild Iraq: the cultural differences that existed between Iraqis and Americans. Indeed, one of the hardest things for Americans to understand was the power various tribes wielded in Iraq. Tribal organization in Iraq dates back thousands of years, to when groups of people who lived in the desert banded together for survival. Those tribal ties and loyalties still exist today. U.S. soldiers discovered that outside of Iraq's big cities, tribal leaders still heavily influence local affairs. They also found out that many tribes are bitter rivals, protective of their own members and wary of people from other tribes. The way the tribes interacted with each other often created tense situations or problems for the soldiers trying to rebuild Iraq.

For example, in October 2003 the 442nd Civil Affairs Battalion chose a local contractor to build five water-pumping stations for the community of Jaafar-Al-Sakar. The pumping stations were necessary to provide water for local residents. A problem arose during construction, however, because the contractor belonged to the al-Jabani tribe. This upset the rival Albu Issa tribe, which demanded that a contractor from their own tribe build the station on their land. The tribal rivalry was so fierce that it almost exploded into violence. Soldier Patricia Weinstein explained what happened:

When we spoke to the contractor [from the al-Jabani tribe], he said he'd been threatened and his men had been told to leave the area. We tried to reason with them that it didn't matter who did it because the whole community would benefit. But we found out it did matter.[83]

The conflict was eventually resolved and soldiers learned a lot about the rivalry that exists between different Iraqi tribes.

Friendship and War

Even though Iraqis and Americans are different in a lot of ways, many members of the military grew to like the Iraqis. This is what navy journalist Farrukh Daniel had to say about Iraqis he met:

The people were awesome. The Iraqi people are the nicest people in the world. They're always smiling, they're giving us presents, little kids are kissing you. We liked to play soccer with the

Abuse at Abu Ghraib

Although American forces were bound by international conventions to treat Iraqi prisoners humanely, in spring 2004 it came to light that terrible abuses had been committed in at least one American-controlled Iraqi detention facility, the prison at Abu Ghraib. Photographs surfaced showing U.S. soldiers posing beside Iraqi prisoners who had been stripped naked and forced into uncomfortable positions or stacked into piles. Other photographs showed naked Iraqis being attacked by police dogs and otherwise terrorized. One hooded prisoner, for example, was photographed balancing on a small box with a noose around his neck and electric wires attached to his hands; the prisoner was reportedly threatened with electrocution if he lowered his arms or fell off the box. Other disturbing reports described the sexual abuse, including rape, of inmates by soldiers.

The abuse of prisoners was decried around the world, and investigations were quickly launched to determine responsibility. It was unclear whether a few rogue soldiers had acted on their own or if the atrocities had been sanctioned by high-ranking military officials. In any case, the prisoner abuse scandal put an uncomfortable spotlight on the behavior of American soldiers in Iraq.

kids. People are people wherever you go. All they wanted to do was be good to their kids, raise a family—just like everybody else.[84]

And giving Iraqis a chance to have a life in which they could raise a family in peace was what thousands of U.S. soldiers were dedicated to doing. Some of them even gave their lives trying to accomplish this goal. Army ma-jor Christopher J. Splinter was one such soldier; he was killed when his vehicle detonated a bomb planted on a road near Samarra. After Splinter was killed, his family released a letter they had received from him in November 2003. In it, Splinter voiced his hope for Iraq's future: "I truly expect this country to be self-sufficient and stable in the next three to five years. Ten years from now, Iraq will be the show state in the Middle East."[85]

Chapter 5

A Constant Threat of Attack

On December 14, 2003, L. Paul Bremer III, the civilian administrator of the Coalition Provisional Authority, made the most significant announcement concerning the Iraq War since President George W. Bush's declaration on May 1 that major combat had ended: "Ladies and gentlemen. We got him!"[86] Bremer's words at a Baghdad news conference were met with cheers and applause by reporters, who knew that "him" was Saddam Hussein, who had eluded soldiers since the fall of Baghdad in April.

Saddam was captured the day before in the town of Abduar, just south of his hometown of Tikrit. Army major general Raymond T. Odierno, commander of the soldiers who made the arrest, said Saddam was discovered in an underground hideout and "was just caught like a rat." Odierno explained why the capture was important: "The intimidation and fear this man generated for over 30 years are now gone. Many will rest much better tonight knowing Iraq is moving forward to a more secure environment."[87]

Among those hoping Saddam's arrest would make Iraq safer were U.S. soldiers. Despite being defeated in the spring of 2003, Iraqis who remained loyal to Saddam continued to launch attacks against U.S. troops. In sporadic hit-and-run guerrilla assaults, they fired rocket-propelled grenades and explosive shells from mortars (small portable cannons) at U.S. forces. Some of them became suicide bombers who strapped explosives to themselves. Others planted bombs along highways and city streets, where they were were detonated by the weight of passing military vehicles.

For many soldiers, this second phase of the Iraq War was worse than the initial six weeks of fighting. Army sergeant Douglas White said of the attacks, "This kind of war is a lot scarier for me." And for Sergeant John Goerger, with the constant threat of danger, he admitted, "I'm more nervous now than I was at the beginning. I know this: People are still dying."[88]

Getting Used to Mortar Shells

Sergeant Tim Hammond was stationed at Camp Sather near Baghdad. Hammond wrote a long e-mail describing his life as a soldier in Iraq. In "An Email from Iraq: Life in the Sandbox" sent to the author in December 2003, he discusses mortar attacks on his base.

Four nights after arriving on base we heard the first mortar attack. It was well away from where we were sleeping but unnerving none the less. I have the impression that the terrorists just lob rocket propelled grenades into the base and really do not have any idea what they are aiming at. . . . Once in a while they get lucky and hit something, not people, close to the edge of the base. I hope their aim never gets any better. These attacks happened about once a week for the first few weeks then only once in a while. The first time it happened I was very nervous and had difficulty sleeping for a couple of nights. A lot of us talked about the attack the next day. The next time it happened I was not quite as nervous as the first. The anxiety became less with each mortar. Now it is to the point where an occasional explosion is just another common sound.

Unconventional Tactics

At the start of the war, the Iraqi army of some 1 million soldiers had seemingly melted away from advancing U.S. and coalition forces, never confronting the invaders in a major battle. But as U.S. soldiers made their way deeper into Iraq, Iraqi soldiers countered with guerrilla-style tactics instead of fighting Americans out in the open. "The enemy has gone asymmetric on us. There are ambushes. It's not conventional,"[89] marine Bryan McCoy said about the fighting. By "asymmetric," McCoy meant that instead of fighting along a defined front, Iraqis were attacking randomly from anywhere.

The enemy, which U.S. officials collectively termed "insurgents," included soldiers of the defeated Iraqi army; Fedayeen, members of a private military group who were personally loyal to Saddam; and civilians from Iraq and neighboring countries who believed the invasion had been wrong. To Americans, the tactics of the insurgents seemed tricky and dishonorable, more like those used by terrorists. Said Army lieutenant colonel Stephen Schiller, "They're not playing by the rules. We play by the rules. It sounds silly in war, but we'd like to think they'd stick by the Geneva Convention [international rules on the conduct of war] and play somewhat fair."[90]

The tactics reminded American soldiers of another conflict four decades earlier. "This is like fighting in Vietnam—little skirmishes everywhere. It's hard to tell who the enemy is out here,"[91] said soldier Mike Pecina. The Vietnam War was a controversial time in U.S. history because it had taken the lives of so many soldiers. Realizing this, Iraq's Deputy Prime Minister Tariq Aziz in April 2003 tried to scare and demoralize U.S. soldiers and citizens by claiming the two wars were alike: "People say to me, 'You are not the Vietnamese. You have no jungles and swamps to hide in.' I reply, 'Let our cities be our swamps and our buildings be our jungles.'"[92]

A Difficult Situation

Taking Aziz's advice, the insurgents used buildings in Iraq's bigger cities to hide in during battles with U.S. soldiers, just as the Vietnamese had concealed themselves in dense jungle foliage. But the way in which the Iraq War most resembled the Vietnam War was that Americans could not always tell if the people they encountered in a combat zone were harmless civilians or enemies ready to kill them. Some fighters disguised themselves as innocent civilians and attacked without warning. Still other insurgents pretended to surrender and then killed their unsuspecting captors.

Such tactics meant that soldiers had to be wary of anyone, even civilians who at first glance appeared harmless. For example, in some situations, Iraqis would approach Americans while waving white flags, indicating they were peaceful. But when the soldiers would relax their guard, the Iraqis would open fire on them with concealed weapons.

Because of such attacks, soldiers were ordered to shoot anyone who failed to heed

At a checkpoint in central Iraq, a patrol unit searches a vehicle and its passengers for weapons.

their warnings to stop before approaching them too closely. But soldiers did not want to kill innocent people. Therefore, routine stops and checkpoints became potentially charged situations. When groups of people or vehicles approached them, soldiers had to make instantaneous decisions about who was threatening and who was harmless. Sergeant Phil Workman and his fellow marines faced one such charged moment when a blue truck neared their checkpoint on the Euphrates River. The vehicle stopped after they issued a warning for it to halt. "When those gentlemen [stopped], they made me happy as pie," Workman said. Corporal Sean Foley was also happy, but he realized the difficult decision he and other soldiers would have had to make if the driver had not obeyed their order. Said Foley, "The last thing I want to do is shoot somebody, but I'm trained to do it. I'm just hoping they're going to listen, that they're going to stop. If not, I have to tell myself to fire and just do it." [93]

At times, the pressure of having to make such split-second decisions led to tragedy. For example, one night while guarding a bridge over the Tigris River, Sergeant Jeff Lujan ordered his men to shoot into the cab of a truck. It looked like a military vehicle, and had refused to stop when ordered. When dawn came, however, it was discovered that the truck had been filled with civilians. Soldiers found a woman and child dead along with signs that others in the truck, mostly men, had fled. Lujan maintained that he had acted correctly to protect his posi-

tion because the vehicle could have been carrying insurgents. "I've reconciled myself," he said. "We did the right thing, even though it was wrong." [94]

The fact that they might have accidentally killed or wounded innocent people was a tremendous emotional burden for many soldiers. One soldier who felt that way was Jeff Mager, a gunner on a tank. While guarding an overpass near Baghdad International Airport, cannon shells he fired destroyed a car and killed two men. When Mager learned days later they were civilians who had failed to heed warnings to stop, he expressed great sorrow. He told a reporter, "Tell them [Iraqis] the fact that I pulled the trigger that killed some of these people makes me very unhappy. Tell them that America did not want things to happen this way. Tell them that I wish that Iraqis will live a better life." [95]

"I Think We're Just Targets"

Most soldiers involved in such incidents felt like Mager. Even though they had invaded Iraq to oust Saddam, they did not want to hurt the civilians who lived there. In fact, U.S. soldiers hoped their victory would help Iraqis have a better life. In the first weeks of the war, many Iraqis hailed American soldiers as liberators of Saddam's oppressive regime. Marine corporal Joe Moore said that he was touched by crowds of Iraqis that cheered arriving soldiers: "It really hit me when we were driving by, seeing all these people waving. This is their Independence Day of sorts. It's a good feeling." [96]

A Rocket Attack

Airman Brian Ferguson was an eyewitness to one of the most famous postwar attacks in Baghdad. Ferguson was in the lobby of the Al Rasheed Hotel on October 26, 2003, when it was hit by several rockets. The attack, which killed one soldier and injured fifteen others, was widely reported because Deputy Secretary of Defense Paul Wolfowitz was staying there. In an air force news release written by John Norgren, Ferguson explains what he saw.

> I was napping on and off in a chair in the lobby. All of a sudden I woke up. I heard whistles, something like a muffled boom. It didn't last long, maybe 30 to 40 seconds. I felt maybe two or three rockets actually hit the building. One was pretty solid; it shook the building. I actually saw two come by the window. It looked like they either (hit) the ground maybe 50 yards from where I was sitting or just flew by the hotel. My first instinct was to take a photograph; my second instinct was to get down. I got down. As soon as the attack was over, there were people in the lobby as quick as you could turn around. I went out into the foyer where everyone had congregated. All of a sudden I (heard) screaming as they (were) bringing (an injured) lady out who had been in one

of the rooms upstairs. After that, it was like a convoy of injured personnel being brought in. It was chaotic at first but [they] restored order very quickly.

The October 2003 rocket attack on the Al Rasheed Hotel in Baghdad injured many and caused extensive damage.

But despite those initial displays of enthusiasm, American troops discovered that many Iraqis resented them, referring to soldiers behind their backs as *Luj*, a swear word that means "beast." And as soldier Shaun Loun also began to realize, the opposition meant continued danger for soldiers. "The war," he admitted, "may be over but it's [still] a violent place."[97]

The threat of violence remained high. As the months went by, the attacks increased. From May 1, 2003, to May 31, 2004, 678 soldiers were killed, compared to 138 who had died during the major combat. And while 550 soldiers had been wounded in March and April 2003, the total for that year topped 2,300, and an additional 2,471 soldiers were wounded in the first five months of 2004. In other words, despite the fact that major combat had been declared over, violence continued to cause casualties as if it were still wartime. The increasing level of attacks led Colonel Christopher Pease to admit in October 2003, "You don't know where or when you're going to be shot at."[98] And in January 2004 Sergeant Latonya Williams claimed, "Everyone's afraid of dying." Sergeant Mercury Goodman declared, "I think we're just targets."[99]

Types of Attacks

The enemy employed many deadly weapons to attack U.S. soldiers—rifles, mortars that fired explosive shells short distances, rocket-propelled grenades, and even missiles and rockets. Many attacks targeted U.S. military bases where soldiers worked and lived. For example, Gregory Sielepkowski said that when he was stationed at Kirkuk Air Base from July to November 2003, the base was often under attack: "They were getting closer. We were [being attacked by] rockets and mortars at least 30 percent of the time. Right before we left [Iraq] they hit us with five rockets right by the chow hall. That was getting close to home. They were honing in."[100]

When security was tightened to make such attacks more difficult, the insurgents began planting bombs—the military called them "improvised explosive devices" (IEDs)—along roads in the countryside and streets in cities. They exploded when military vehicles ran over them or soldiers stepped on the IEDs. Because it was very difficult to spot such devices, there was little soldiers could do to defend themselves, and there were soon so many of them that it made life difficult and hazardous. Army specialist Ciria Crawford explained that by October, travel in Baghdad was always dangerous: "There have been numerous IEDs around the area during the time we have been working here. We had to adjust the route to get here safely and have traveled down many alleyways where rocks were thrown at us."[101]

Insurgents next began targeting helicopters. On November 2, 2003, insurgents used a ground-to-air missile to shoot down a helicopter near Fallujah, killing sixteen soldiers and wounding twenty more. It was the deadliest attack on American troops since the Iraq War had begun. Several more helicopters were shot down in the next few months, and one such attack on January 8, 2004, killed nine soldiers near Fallujah. Scott Alan Timm, a survivor of the attack, explained what it was like to be shot down. Interviewed by a military journalist before being wheeled into surgery for bruises and lacerations to his face and head, Timm said, "I remember seeing a missile hit the rear turbine [engine]. I thought it was an RPG [rocket-propelled grenade]. The helicopter started bucking wildly in the back, then there was this big fireball, and everybody was trying to get me out."[102]

On November 7, six soldiers died when another helicopter went down along the Tigris River near Tikrit, a center for anti-American sentiment. U.S. troops retaliated by rolling through the city in armored vehicles and firing machine guns and heavy weapons to blast homes suspected of being hideouts for insurgents.

"The Wild, Wild West"

The random nature of the attacks forced the U.S. military to change the way it trained its soldiers. Because support troops such as truck drivers, mechanics, and cooks were usually far behind the battle lines and not involved in fighting, they initially received minimal combat training. But after months of attacks by insurgents, such soldiers stationed in Iraq were ordered to sharpen their shooting and other combat skills because they, too, were in danger. Army general Mark Herling, who commanded troops in Baghdad, explained why that was necessary: "I don't think there are any 'behind-the-lines' anymore. There's no more onlookers on the battlefield."[103]

Even truck drivers hauling something as harmless as medical supplies or food faced a

A car burns in Baghdad. It was driven by a suicide bomber who failed in his attack on U.S. soldiers.

constant threat from hidden IEDs, which could explode at any time when the vehicles were traveling. This changed a job that was normally routine to one that was dangerous. As Colonel John Christenson explained, "Every [transportation] operation is a combat operation. We go out with our Rambo face on. This is still the wild, wild west out here."[104]

In one such incident on November 23, 2003, two army soldiers were driving a civilian vehicle through Mosul when shots were fired into their car, sending it crashing into a wall. A dozen teenagers pulled them from the wreckage and beat them to death with concrete blocks while onlookers stole their weapons and personal belongings. Because military officials did not learn about the attack right away, the bodies of the dead soldiers lay in the street for over an hour.

To counter the increasing number of deadly attacks, the military established safe areas around their facilities by erecting concrete barriers. This made it harder for vehicles containing explosives or armed insurgents to get close enough to attack. More guards were also put on duty outside potential targets. But Air Force Reserve captain Tim Martz, a security specialist, said it was impossible to protect soldiers all the time: "I don't think there are any 100 percent foolproof security plans. Terrorists are very creative and [they] spend a lot of time planning. You do the best you can to try to minimize the threat. That's all you can do."[105]

The military also issued more body armor to its soldiers to reduce wounds and deaths. Soldiers were given body vests made of Kevlar plates, which weighed sixteen pounds. The vests made soldiers hotter in a climate that was already uncomfortably warm. But they were worth the discomfort because they could deflect bullets and shrapnel, the sharp, deadly bits of metal created when mortar shells and other explosive devices detonate.

This type of gear protected Sergeant Patrick Brown on October 27, 2003, when a rocket-propelled grenade struck his Humvee in Baghdad. He was wounded in the legs, right shoulder, cheek, and chin. Brown credited the armor with protecting vital areas like his chest, allowing him to escape more serious injury or even death. "If you notice where my wounds are, the shrapnel is basically where the vest didn't cover,"[106] he said.

Searching for the Enemy

The most aggressive tactic to protect soldiers was to hunt down those attacking them. In operations with forceful names like Iron Hammer, Ivy Cyclone, and Rifle Blitz, soldiers targeted areas or homes in which they hoped to seize weapons or insurgents. Such raids were dangerous, however, because soldiers never knew when they would encounter danger. Said Colonel Christopher Pease, "Every time you do a knock and search, it's a combat operation. You don't know where or when you're going to be shot at."[107]

The anti-American resistance was especially strong in and around Tikrit, Saddam

Going on a Raid

While in Iraq from January to August 2003, Navy journalist Farrukh Daniel wrote stories about many of the tasks military personnel performed. To do research for his stories, Daniel often went with soldiers on missions. In an interview with the author, the navy reservist explained what it was like to go along on a raid in the city of Karbala.

The raids were mostly to look for arms or when we had a tip that a Baath Party official or a member of the Fedayeen was there. It was usually just a single home. You would go so you could search the house or interrogate someone. As a [military] journalist, you have to go along and do what everybody else is doing. So

I've been on raids, I've had to chase guys down, tackle guys, and zip-tie [put plastic handcuffs on] guys. Over there, they're just like people in America if the cops show up here and they're afraid of something. Everybody runs for it. I'm on this one raid and when we go into the house they start flying out of all the exits. This one guy takes off. He doesn't want to go to jail and he's running fast. I finally catch up to him. But I've been chasing him and I really don't know where I'm at any more. Here I am, I've got this guy, and I'm alone in some alley in a city in Iraq. I had no idea where I was and I'm trying to figure out how to get back to the house and the others I came with. It was scary.

Hussein's hometown. Army specialist Moses Rodriguez talked about the dangers of conducting such missions in the area, which was a center of insurgent activity. "There's times you go down those dark, dark alleys with holes in [the walls of nearby buildings] and open windows. One AK [machine-gun burst] through a hole and you're gone,"[108] Rodriguez said. Rodriguez made those comments to a reporter on September 23, 2003, while he and other members of the Fourth Infantry Division were riding in Humvees down one of those dangerous alleys. Their mission that day was to arrest civilian suspected of channeling money to insurgents.

When the soldiers reached the suspect's house, they smashed in a steel gate and the front door of the home to make the arrest. While a helicopter kept watch from above, soldiers in alleys and streets surrounded the house so no one could escape. The raid went

smoothly, but afterward soldiers just wanted to forget about the tense, potentially dangerous situation they had just endured. "I call home and talk to my family and just don't talk about it," said Sergeant Lonnie Henton. Rodriguez also wanted to put the raid out of his mind. "I don't think about it. I just write my family,"[109] he said.

Soldiers who went on such raids believed their missions were important because they were eliminating insurgents who were harming soldiers and Iraqi civilians. Before one group of soldiers departed on a raid on October 31, 2003, a chaplain asked them to pray with him. Bowing his head, he said, "Lord, there are bad guys out there. Just help us kill 'em."[110] The prayer might sound cruel to someone whose life has not been in danger on a daily basis for months. But for soldiers who had become targets of constant attack, the focus of the raid—in fact, their entire tour of duty in Iraq—had come down to one simple reality: kill or be killed.

Getting Saddam

The most notable raid of the postwar period was no doubt the one that led to the capture of Saddam Hussein. Much emphasis was placed on his capture because many

Former Iraqi leader Saddam Hussein after his capture. He had grown a bushy beard as a disguise.

Iraqis were still worried he could somehow regain control of the country. Thus until Saddam was captured, many Iraqis were afraid to cooperate with the Americans because they thought they would be punished if he ever returned to power.

Saddam had fled Baghdad in April 2003 when U.S. and coalition forces captured Iraq's capital, and for months he remained the most wanted man in Iraq. Saddam even managed to make several audiotapes that, when played on the radio, gave hope to his supporters that he could return in triumph to lead the country. Although U.S. officials believed Saddam was hiding out near Tikrit, they could not pinpoint his exact location. But on December 12, officials were tipped off by an Iraqi citizen who told them that Saddam was hiding near the town of Abduar. In a mission code-named Operation Red Dawn, six hundred soldiers commanded by Colonel James Hickey went to both locations the next day.

At about 6 P.M. on December 13, the soldiers began searching a small farmhouse at one of the sites. The one-story home made of concrete blocks was empty, but a soldier noticed a piece of fiber sticking out of the dirt in the house's courtyard. When several soldiers pulled on the material, a small rug emerged. It was covering a plastic foam panel, which served as a cover for an underground chamber.

Fearing someone would emerge to attack them, soldiers prepared to throw a grenade down the hole when two hands suddenly came into view. Soldiers pulled out a man with a wild, tangled beard. To their amazement, the man said in English, "I am Saddam Hussein, president of Iraq. I am willing to negotiate." A soldier replied jokingly, "President Bush sends his regards."[111]

The powerful dictator had been hiding in what Lieutenant General Ricardo Sanchez, commander of coalition forces, would later call a "spider hole." The underground chamber was about six to eight feet deep, with just enough space for a person to lie down. In the hut where Saddam stayed when he was not in the hole, soldiers found two rifles, a pistol, and $750,000 in U.S. currency.

For those who helped arrest Saddam, and for soldiers stationed all over Iraq, it was a great day. Said soldier Michael Tillery, "It feels good. All the work has paid off and that one step [toward pacifying Iraq] is finally over—finding Saddam."[112] As of mid-2004, however, the insurgency was still active, and Iraq continued to be a dangerous place for American soldiers.

Chapter 6

Iraq: A Difficult Place to Serve

The hardest part about being stationed in Iraq for U.S. soldiers was the long-distance separation from family and friends. Fathers and mothers hated being away from their children, wives and husbands longed for their spouses, sons and daughters missed their parents, and everyone had friends they wished they could see again. The feelings of sadness and loneliness soldiers experienced because of this were never sharper than during holidays, when loved ones would gather together to celebrate those special occasions.

Despite being far from home, some American soldiers did everything they could to bring holiday sights and sounds to their station in the desert. One such soldier was Rebecca Burt, who worked hard to make the 2003 Christmas holiday an event that Christian soldiers could enjoy even from Iraq. Burt expected that many other soldiers, like herself, would have a tough time getting through the holiday while being far from home: "We have young guys away from mom and dad for the first [time] and older married guys who are having a really hard time knowing that their children won't be waking them up early Christmas morning."[113]

To help bring Christmas to Iraq, Burt asked friends and family members to send her decorations to provide soldiers with the day's familiar sights. She received five artificial trees and boxes of ornaments, which she handed out to various units so they could celebrate the holiday. "A tree definitely helps to instill a little Christmas spirit," Burt said. "[Christmas spirit] is something that can be hard to come by if you're used to snow and [are] suddenly looking at sand and palm trees!"[114] Burt also decorated offices and other areas with "Merry Christmas" signs and paper snowflakes. On Christmas Eve and Christmas Day she visited guard stations to hand out candy canes to soldiers.

The Christmas celebrations Burt and soldiers in other units organized briefly brought a touch of home to Iraq. This was a welcome change, because to soldiers Iraq was often a strange, inhospitable, and unsettling place to serve their country. It was also one in which circumstances forced them to live uncomfortably, and to have to do without amenities they had taken for granted back home.

A Strange Land

Although the soldiers who went to Iraq knew they would see and experience many new things, most were unprepared for how vastly different life in that country was compared to what they were accustomed to at home. Life in big cities like Baghdad seemed somewhat familiar to U.S. soldiers because there were modern buildings and lots of cars, and its residents enjoyed conveniences such as electricity and indoor plumbing. But many American soldiers were amazed at the way people lived in the rural areas of Iraq. Many

of these people had no electricity. They obtained their water from wells dug by hand, traveled by riding donkeys, and lived in simple dwellings made of dried mud.

To many soldiers, being in these parts of Iraq was a surreal experience. Compared with the wealthy, technological world they had left behind at home, rural Iraq was a very poor place in which many people lived simply and primitively. One marine, Omar Monge, felt like he had traveled through time when he saw a donkey tied next to a home made of mud bricks in Al Qadisiya. He commented in amazement, "This is a place taken out of thousands of years ago when Jesus was walking the earth still."[115] Navy journalist Farrukh Daniel felt similarly. The difference in the way rural Iraqis lived became dramatically apparent to him when his truck convoy met up with sheep being

Field Afar

The baseball was a tennis ball wrapped in toilet paper and duct tape, the bases paper plates, and the playing field hot tarmac, not sweet-smelling green grass. Also, the games could be played only at night because it was too hot for such an athletic event during the day. But for soldiers in the 101st Airborne Division, the baseball diamond they built in the desert named "Field Afar" was a treasured site. In a story in *Sports Illustrated,* columnist Rick Reilly explains that the rough playing field was important to soldiers because it helped them relax:

> [It was a special place even to] guys like specialist Ronald Hancock of Alpha Company, who doesn't play baseball but spends his

downtime at the field keeping score. "It gives me something to do," he says. "It keeps my mind off the fact that [soldiers sometimes worry] we're never going home."

As Reilly pointed out, however, the soldiers did have something real to worry about: the constant possibility of attack. But even though glaring lights that turned the night into day might have made the soldier–baseball players easy targets, they still wanted to play ball because it took their minds off what they were enduring by being stationed in Iraq. As Captain Adam Kamann put it, "It [the danger] does make us a little nervous, but we're all too engrossed in the game to worry about all the what-ifs."

driven by shepherds with wooden crooks. Daniel described his impressions of the scene: "Those sheep herders were walking their sheep across the road just like their ancestors had been walking sheep across that road for the last two thousand years. It was like a scene right out of the Bible."[116]

Other aspects of life in rural Iraq challenged many soldiers. For example, it was common to see heavy, smelly smoke from burning tires darkening the sky at all hours of the day. Although the smell bothered the soldiers, burning tires was one of the only ways some poor Iraqis could warm themselves or cook their food. In a country heavily damaged by war, many Iraqis for months lived in substandard shelter, lacked decent food and clean water, and had to make do without electricity and other amenities that made life easier. Exposure to such poverty was new and shocking to many American soldiers.

Poor Living Conditions

However, U.S. forces experienced their share of primitive living conditions as well. At both temporary and permanent bases, soldiers often had to do without basic comforts that most Americans take for granted. Living in these conditions was a new and difficult challenge for many soldiers, and contributed to feelings of loneliness, isolation, and homesickness.

U.S. military bases had various levels of comfort. They had different facilities depending on how many soldiers they housed. The smallest, home to only a handful of sol-

diers, usually had no hot meals, no running water, no toilets, and no air conditioning. There were usually few, if any, leisure activities to help soldiers relax.

In some places, living conditions were so bad that no soldier wanted to remain there longer than necessary. "Truck drivers," said one soldier, "would rather stay on the road than be in camp. As fast as they came back, they wanted to roll out again."[117] Exemplary of such a place was Bashur Airfield, an air force base 255 miles north of Baghdad. Describing Bashur as "a dump with a 7,000-foot runway," Airman Louis A. Arana-Barradas said the base lived up to a description another airman had given him upon his arrival:

> He said something like, "Welcome to Bashur. It's a war zone. It's noisy. Dusty when it's dry. Muddy when it rains. There are no toilets. No showers. No electricity. No heat. No running water. No buildings. No McDonalds. Questions?"[118]

Indeed, even after major combat ended, many camps and bases were still miserable places to live. Even by late May, living conditions had not improved very much in Baghdad, where the U.S. military was headquartered. At Baghdad International Airport—formerly Saddam International Airport until its capture by U.S. soldiers—members of the U.S. Army's First Armored Division slept on cots in a large building in which nearly every window was broken. And although the open windows provided some relief from the heat by allowing ventilation, Lieutenant

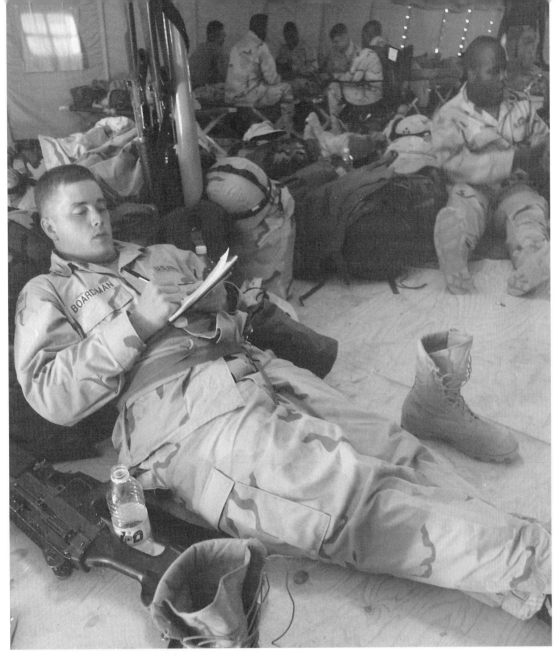

To help cope with separation from friends and family, soldiers in Iraq often wrote letters home.

Colonel John McGrath said they were more of a nuisance than a blessing: "The dust blows through [them]. The pigeons fly in and crap on your stuff."[119]

Mealtime was another occasion for soldiers to miss the comforts of home. Sergeant Gregory Sielepkowski, an air force reservist who was stationed at Kirkuk Air Base, described the "chow" as being at times inedible. Although there was generally a lot of food, soldiers stationed at Kirkuk were not

Iraqi Palaces

Air Force Reserve captain Tim Martz was in Iraq in April and May 2003 setting up security procedures for military bases and other locations. As part of his job, he visited many luxurious palaces that had been built for Saddam Hussein and other leaders. In fact, he slept in one with other military personnel. In an interview with the author, Martz described the palaces.

We were actually based in one of the palaces of the former regime [in Baghdad]. There was such a stark contrast between the way the average Iraqi citizen lived versus the regime—the Baath Party officials, Saddam, his sons—and how they lived. My assignment took me to various locations around Baghdad, so I saw a lot of the palaces. They were very elaborate.

Everything was ornate marble—the staircases, floors, the ceilings in both the palaces and sub-palaces [smaller ones in the same complex]. You could tell that a lot of money and effort went into them, especially those for Saddam and his family. They had indoor swimming pools, outdoor swimming pools, and man-made lakes. Many were big complexes with a large palace or series of palaces and smaller elaborate guesthouses. Beyond them were poor areas that contrasted sharply with the palaces I saw.

Two soldiers stand guard at one of Saddam Hussein's many lavish palaces.

served many fresh vegetables or fruit, and the meat they had was not very good. In fact, soldiers often had trouble identifying just what kind of meat it was. Said Sielepkowski of his dining experience, "I was getting sick from the chow hall food. A lot of us got pretty sick. I don't know if it was [from the] water it was cooked in or what."[120]

In larger and more permanent facilities, however, conditions gradually improved through 2003 and 2004. The conditions in larger camps in particular got better. Camps that were home to several thousand soldiers might have a dining hall that offered hot meals. They were usually equipped with showers and indoor toilets. Many had a post exchange (PX) where soldiers could buy snacks and other items. These bases also offered a wide range of off-duty entertainment, including Internet access and movies. The biggest bases, home to twenty thousand or more military personnel and civilian workers, might even have swimming pools or gyms in which soldiers could keep fit. These facilities also featured live shows by entertainers from America. Best of all, these bases were usually entirely air conditioned.

Some military personnel stationed in Iraq did not stay in military bases at all. In fact, they were quartered not in tents or even wooden barracks but in one of the hundreds of lavish palaces scattered throughout Iraq that had been built for Saddam Hussein and other leaders. Air Force Reserve captain Tim Martz remembers a palace in Baghdad he lived in in April 2003:

It had a big ballroom with a huge chandelier, three or four stories high. It was pretty incredible. We set up our cots in there and our mosquito netting and pretty much made a barracks out of a big ballroom. We had electricity from a generator in one palace and we watched TV.[121]

It was a unique experience to stay in a palace. But soldiers who did so would have traded such lavish quarters for the humblest dwelling back home so they could be with their loved ones once again.

Lonely in Iraq

The substandard living conditions soldiers often endured were easier to take than being thousands of miles away from all the people who were important in their lives. And the longer they were away, the more they missed them. Realizing what a burden this was, the military did what it could to help soldiers deal with their loneliness by speeding up mail delivery, setting up Internet service, and having "morale phones" on which soldiers could call home.

The Iraq War was America's first war in which most people had Internet access. For many soldiers, e-mails, which could be transmitted instantaneously, became the favored form of communication. Navy reservist Gary Kernodle admitted he had never been more thankful for computers than when he was in Iraq from March to August 2003:

At first it [communication] was through letters, which was slow going. But later they had e-mail set up. I tell you, that was a big deal there. That helped out a lot. That was pretty much a daily routine, getting your e-mail. It was nice to hear from home. E-mail was better than letters, really.[122]

But communicating with loved ones was not the same as being with them, especially during important family occasions. For example, when Sergeant Jeff Bush and the rest of the army's Third Infantry began advancing into Iraq on March 20, 2003, he was saddened to realize that it was the same day as his daughter's second birthday. As the weeks and months went by, Bush missed his daughter and wife more and more. At times, he would sit back and dream about what it would be like to be with his family again: "I picture being together with [my daughter] and my wife at the park, riding the little horse with the springs or going on the slide. I picture her in the morning calling my name, and picking her up."[123]

The loneliness intensified for many soldiers when something sad happened back home, such as an injury or death of a loved one. Soldiers felt helpless because they were too far away to do anything. Conversely, even a joyous event could sadden them because they could not be at home to share it. That was the case for hundreds of soldiers who became fathers while serving in Iraq. One of them was Sergeant William Sanchez, a member of the Florida National Guard whose son was born in August 2003.

"At a Moment's Notice"

For Sanchez and other members of part-time service units such as the National Guard or reserve, being stationed in Iraq entailed other hardships besides being away from loved ones. For these service men and women, being ordered to Iraq included the added shock of having to transform into full-time soldiers in just a few weeks. Sanchez said in many ways the Iraq War was tougher on part-time soldiers: "The National Guard has a harder time than the regular Army in this kind of deployment. A lot of guys have left their families at a moment's notice, their wives pregnant, newborn babies, new jobs, new houses."[124]

An extra problem for such part-time soldiers was that their military salary was usually less than what they earned at their civilian jobs as bankers, policemen, factory workers, or teachers. A few employers such as state and local government agencies made up the pay disparity for workers who were called up for the war. But for many part-time soldiers, the reduced earnings caused financial problems for their families, who now had less money to live on and pay bills.

Typical of such financial setbacks was the experience of Jim Larson, a Wisconsin air national guardsman who at home was a Wisconsin state trooper. Larson had been called up for active duty early in 2002 and served in Iraq until June 2003. The financial losses he suffered while being on active duty forced him to use savings set aside for the education of his daughter to pay family bills. Said Larson:

A soldier in the National Guard loads toys for Iraqi children. Many members of the National Guard were deployed to Iraq on a moment's notice.

I'm living a life where I'm used to earning more, and I know, I put myself in this situation when I enlisted, but all of a sudden I have a severe reduction in pay. There were bills that lagged behind, bill collectors were calling, and your credit record gets tarnished.[125]

It was hard for soldiers to see their finances deteriorate while they were serving their country. Concern over such personal

Not Much to Do

Soldiers stationed in Iraq often became bored because they did not have many recreational opportunities. While stationed at Camp Sather in 2003, Air Force technical sergeant Tim Hammond filled his downtime by writing about his experiences. In "An Email from Iraq: Life in the Sandbox," Hammond discussed recreation in a war zone.

In our off time there are not a lot of things to do here. There is a facility to watch television or play video games, play cards or board games. There is a quiet area to read, write letters or just relax. There is a weight lifting facility, and a large tent with a nice assortment of [other exercise] equipment. Anyone can walk or run outside in day light if they choose. This is not the greatest place to run because the ground is covered mostly with loose gravel and sand. Besides those things there is always a constant light haze of dust in the air. Many people read and write letters home or spend time on computers emailing. Everyone has their thing to do to pass the time. In the evening I spend time on this epic email. I should mention at this point some of the things we do to combat evening boredom. Rock throwing games seem to happen quite frequently. Someone may finish a bottle of water, throw the empty onto the gravel and that could easily trigger a good half hour or more of rock throwing. The games are almost like being a kid again. We throw rocks trying to hit certain objects, sometimes out of our reach and certainly always above our skill level. Some people are better than others.

problems was only one of many issues that, as the months went by, led many U.S. soldiers to become angry, unhappy, and even depressed.

Unhappy in Iraq

For American soldiers, there were many uncomfortable, unpleasant things about serving in Iraq—the spartan, sometimes primitive living conditions, long workdays in a dangerous and hostile environment, lack of opportunities to relax and have fun, and separation from family and friends. Added to that was the uncertainty of when they would be going home, a timetable that kept being pushed back for many soldiers because of continued armed resistance to U.S. forces. By the summer of 2003, all of these issues had combined to weaken morale among U.S. troops serving in Iraq.

Speaking anonymously to a reporter in July 2003, one officer with the Third Infantry Division summed up the mood of the military: "Make no mistake, the level of morale for most soldiers that I've seen has hit rock bottom."[126] The military newspaper *Stars and Stripes* confirmed that assessment when it interviewed some two thousand soldiers throughout Iraq. In a survey about personal morale, 34 percent of soldiers rated it "low" or "very low," 27 percent "high" or "very high," and the rest "average."

Americans at home were surprised to hear reports that some soldiers were feeling unhappy after having so easily won the war. But these soldiers were experiencing what is known as combat fatigue, a military term for the fear, guilt, and other negative emotions many of them had stored up during fighting.

Symptoms of combat fatigue include sadness, fear of the future, and general depression.

Many other soldiers were also depressed simply because they missed loved ones. The most common symptom of depression is that people lack energy and can sleep for hours and hours. Some soldiers, however, like Joe Cruz, had the opposite problem—they had trouble sleeping. "I wake up in the middle of the night just to look around. I am always half-asleep," he said. Cruz had been away from his family for a year, and his loneliness had begun to lead to depression. "When I get depressed, I just write a letter [to my mom]," he said. "I write a lot. Writing a letter relieves my stress." [127]

Suicide

Some soldiers simply could not handle the stress and other negative emotions they experienced. In 2003 at least twenty-one soldiers stationed in Iraq committed suicide. Military officials said the main reason the soldiers killed themselves was that they desperately wanted to go home, either because they were lonely or because they felt they needed to go back to handle family problems. One soldier killed himself after talking with his wife on the telephone. Witnesses who heard the call said the soldier was upset about being away from home while a problem unfolded there. He reportedly said, "There is nothing I can do from here." [128] After the soldier hung up, he shot himself in the head with his revolver.

Some of the soldiers who died, however, may not have been trying to commit suicide.

Instead, it is believed that some of the men and women who killed themselves were trying only to wound themselves seriously enough so they would be sent home. In Tikrit, Army captain Justin Cole had to deal with two soldiers who died after shooting themselves; one man shot himself in the leg, striking an artery, and a woman shot herself in the stomach. After an investigation into the deaths, Cole said he believed the deaths were unintentional: "I think they were missing home, very much wanting to go home and as a result did harm to themselves. Unfortunately they did pass away." [129]

To ease the emotional anguish of many soldiers, in the fall of 2003 U.S. officials began rotating soldiers home on leave—the one thing they all desperately wanted.

Visits Home

The first soldiers to receive the two-week leaves were the ones who had been away the longest. The first leaves were granted in September 2003. For Army private Larry Burns, being back meant being able to see and hold his two-week-old daughter, Alexia, for the first time. "It's good to be back. My wife just had a baby and I'm really looking forward to seeing her," [130] he said.

Some families adjusted the calendar to celebrate birthdays and holidays around the time when soldiers were able to be home to share the special occasions. For example, in 2003 the Witmer family of New Berlin, Wisconsin, celebrated Christmas on December 9 because sisters Michelle and Rachel, members of the Wisconsin National

Guard, were home after having served in Baghdad since March. Although they headed back to Iraq before Christmas Day, they were delighted to be home. "You value every moment. It's a gift,"[131] said Michelle Witmer. Michelle was killed in Baghdad April 9, 2004, when the vehicle in which she was riding was attacked. A third sister, Charity Witmer, was also serving in Iraq at the time.

Another soldier who got one of the morale-boosting passes was Daniel Hendrix, who flew home to Colorado in October 2003 to witness the birth of Matthew Lee, his first child. During the brief visit with his family, he changed diapers for the first time in his life. Hendrix soon had to head back to Iraq

to resume his service. Coming home for such a short visit was jarring for him. "Over there you carry a weapon all the time. Here I'm carrying my baby. It's a big switch,"[132] he said.

When soldiers did return to Iraq, they had to find relief from the pressure of being there in any small, unexpected joys that came their way. For some soldiers, that came on Thanksgiving Day 2003.

Giving Thanks

The military always tries to give soldiers a special meal on holidays. In 2003, some six

During his surprise Thanksgiving visit in 2003, President Bush meets U.S. soldiers in Baghdad.

hundred soldiers in Baghdad had a Thanksgiving that was extraordinary not because it included hot turkey with all the trimmings but because President George W. Bush flew in secretly to help them celebrate. The men and women in the dining hall when the president arrived were as surprised as people throughout the world were the next day when they heard about the visit by Bush, who as commander in chief of the armed forces was the soldiers' superior officer as well as their president.

Although Bush's visit was criticized by some as a political stunt to boost his popularity, soldiers were impressed that he traveled halfway around the world to be with them. Sergeant Gerrie Holland summed up the feelings of many: "It's not easy being here. Every day you're over here, you feel depressed anyway. But it's especially hard on a holiday. It shows that he cares about us and is thinking about us." Army private Stephen Henderson was not only surprised but delighted: "I feel uplifted. I almost forgot I was even here." [133]

And being able to forget Iraq, even for a moment, was a blessed relief for every soldier.

The Iraq War Changes Their Lives Forever

No soldier who served in the Iraq War returned home the same. What was seen and experienced in that far-off land changed every man and woman who went there. Although some returned with physical injuries that would affect them the rest of their lives, for most soldiers the transformations were more subtle than a lost limb or a scar. The changes were very personal; many soldiers came home with new attitudes and complex emotions.

Sergeant Tracy Fisher experienced such changes in simple acts, such as listening to Jimi Hendrix's wailing guitar version of the "Star-Spangled Banner," which her mother had sent her while she was serving in Baghdad in 2003. Fisher said that after having gone to war for her country, America's national anthem meant more to her than ever before: "Now I get chills listening to it. Millions and millions of people fought many battles for America to be what it is. Now I'm part of that fight for the right of others to be free." Fisher realized her life would never be the same after her experience in the military. "When I get back, I'm basically starting my life over,"[134] she said while still in Baghdad. It would be the same for many veterans of the Iraq War.

Combat Affects Soldiers

The soldiers most deeply affected by the war were those who were in combat. Lieutenant Colonel Ken Brown, a chaplain with the U.S. Army's 101st Airborne Division, believes combat transformed everyone because of the powerful emotions it stirs up. After counseling soldiers following the first violent weeks of the war, Brown said:

> I think you see significant change in young people who face death—their priorities change. I had a young man come to me a couple of weeks ago that had seen a soldier killed. [His feelings were] something that I faced as a young man in Vietnam as an infantryman—that is, you're guilty you're alive and your buddy

is dead. All I did was just say, "Well, you may come to the conclusion that God has spared you in this particular instance. Now what are you going to do with that life that you have now?"[135]

Indeed, combat in the Iraq War left indelible marks on everyone who endured it.

Many soldiers gained new confidence in themselves because they had successfully met the most difficult challenge they had ever faced. Some soldiers, horrified by the

Wounded soldiers are loaded on a plane at Baghdad International Airport for their long flight home.

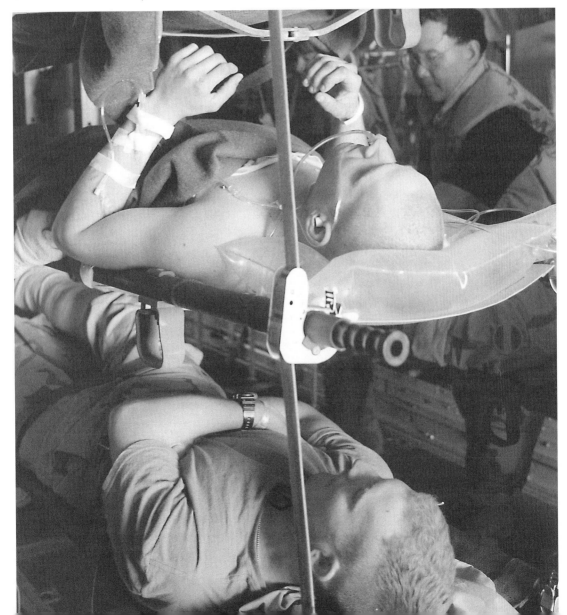

death and destruction they saw, came away with a new appreciation for life. Many others were so overwhelmed by the realities of war that they would be haunted the rest of their lives. Twenty-one-year-old Kyle Hetcel said he will relive his battle memories forever:

> I have some nightmares [about combat situations]. . . . I wake up in a cold sweat every now and then. I realize [then that] this is just a dream. This is my first war, and it has an effect on everybody. That's why I have these nightmares. And they will probably be stuck with me for the rest of my life.[136]

The Injured

For some veterans, the effects of the Iraq War were more tangible than nightmares. For hundreds of soldiers, combat left scars that were physical, not psychological. Serious wounds and injuries shattered not only their bodies but their futures. For example, Sergeant Matthew Dewitt lost both of his hands when a rocket-propelled grenade struck the Humvee he was riding in. While recuperating at Walter Reed Army Medical Center in Washington, D.C., Dewitt admitted he was unsure what the future held for him: "I don't know what I'll do. I don't know what's there for me to do now."[137]

Many soldiers were treated at Walter Reed for life-altering injuries they suffered in the Iraq War. Although many wondered what turn their lives would take because of the injuries they had suffered, most were able to face the future with bravery. Alan Jermaine Lewis, for example, who lost both his legs when a land mine exploded under him in Baghdad, exhibited extreme courage when considering his future. Even though he had to learn to walk all over again on artificial legs, Lewis was grateful just to be alive:

> I try not to feel sad for myself, because there's a lot of soldiers who are in a lot worse condition than I am. I know a guy who lost his arm and both legs. So I gotta be thankful for what I have. I'm just thankful to be alive, and I thank [God] for what he's done for me.[138]

Lewis realized he was lucky he did not have to make the ultimate sacrifice for his country—giving up his life. But hundreds of soldiers did die in the Iraq War. One of them was Kirk Straseskie, who drowned on May 19, 2003, while trying to rescue fellow marines after their helicopter crashed into a canal. During his funeral in Beaver Dam, Wisconsin, a friend read a letter the marine had written him several years earlier. In the letter, Straseskie explained that if he was killed in the line of duty, it would not be in vain:

> I do not want to die, it saddens me to think of what I would miss if I were killed. But don't confuse that with fear. I am not afraid to die, and I am prepared to in both my heart and my soul. It is my belief that there are greater causes to live and fight for than one's self. That is why I serve.[139]

A Poem to His Dad

Many men and women who served in Iraq felt the same way as Straseskie. And although most soldiers were not killed or seriously wounded, they all sacrificed a great deal by fighting in a foreign country far from their loved ones.

In 2003 when Sergeant Mike Ashby was stationed in Iraq, his eight-year-old son Chase wrote him a poem. Titled simply "Air Force," it reads:

Willing to do their job,

Willing to serve our country.

They fight our wars,

And give us freedom.

My Dad does all that. [140]

The poem is a bittersweet reminder of the sacrifices made by U.S. soldiers during the Iraq War, one they and many Americans will likely never forget.

☆ Notes ☆

Introduction: Why They Were There

1. Ricardo Sanchez, Coalition Provisional Authority press briefing, November 11, 2003. Transcript by Federal News Service Inc. www.centcom.mil/Centcom News/Transcripts/20031101.htm.
2. Paige Augustino, interview with author, Milwaukee, WI, November 20, 2003.
3. Quoted in Larry Stevens, "Mother of Six Serves as Operation Iraqi Freedom Truck Driver," October 31, 2003. www.defenselink.mil/news/Oct2003.
4. Quoted in Stevens, "Mother of Six Serves as Operation Iraqi Freedom Truck Driver."
5. Quoted in Drew Brown, "Among the Infantry a Gritty, Hot Life with a Few Simple Pleasures," *Stars and Stripes,* March 19, 2003. www.stripes.com.
6. Quoted in Steve Liewer, "Wounded Soldiers Recount Harried Moments on the Battlefield," *Stars and Stripes,* April 10, 2003. www.stripes.com.
7. Quoted in Liewer, "Wounded Soldiers Recount Harried Moments on the Battlefield."
8. Quoted in Simon Robinson, "The Insurgent and the Soldier," *Time,* November 17, 2003, p. 48.
9. Leonard Wong et al., "Why They Fight: Combat Motivation in the Iraq War," Strategic Studies Institute, September 2003. www.army.mil/prof_writing/volumes/volume1/september_2003/9_03_1.html.

Chapter 1: Preparing for War

10. Quoted in Russ Bynum, "Troops Deploy from Across U.S. to Gulf," Associated Press, January 7, 2003, in *NewsBank Special Report: Postwar Iraq.* www.info web.newsbank.com.
11. Quoted in Nancy Gibbs, "Moving Out," *Time,* January 27, 2003, p. 34.
12. Quoted in Laura Coleman Noeth, "If War Is Hell, So Is Separation," *Commercial Appeal,* January 27, 2003, p. A1.
13. Quoted in Gibbs, "Moving Out," p. 35.
14. Quoted in Bynum, "Troops Deploy from Across U.S. to Gulf."
15. Quoted in Nancy Gibbs, "An American Family Goes to War," *Time,* March 24, 2003.
16. Paul Hartje interview with author, Milwaukee, WI, November 20, 2003.
17. Quoted in Jeremy M. Vought, "Food on the Go!" 1st Force Service Support Group, March 4, 2003. www.usmc.mil.
18. Quoted in Roger Roy, "Delays Burden Marines in Kuwait," *Orlando Sentinel,* March 14, 2003, p. A1.

19. Quoted in Kit T. Roane, "Dug In Far from Home," *U.S. News & World Report,* March 10, 2003, p. 26.

20. Quoted in Nahal Toosi, "Reading, Writing, and Waiting for War," *Milwaukee Journal-Sentinel,* March 14, 2003, p. 1A.

21. Quoted in Jeremy M. Vought, "Rodeo Kicks Up Sand in Kuwaiti Desert," 1st Force Service Support Group, March 23, 2003. www.usmc.mil.

22. Quoted in Ann Scott Tyson, "Sands of Time Pass Slowly for Soldiers Poised in Kuwait," *Christian Science Monitor,* March 13, 2003, p. 4.

23. Farrukh Daniel, interview with author, Milwaukee, WI, December 13, 2003.

24. Quoted in Evan Thomas, "Fear at the Front," *Newsweek,* February 3, 2003, p. 35.

25. Quoted in Drew Brown, "On Eve of War, Infantrymen Wage Private Battles," *Stars and Stripes,* March 18, 2003. www.stripes.com.

26. Quoted in Ron Martz, "Troops Sense War Near," *Atlanta Journal-Constitution,* March 13, 2003, p. A1.

27. Quoted in Mary Beth Sheridan, "'This Is the Real Live Stuff, Ladies," *Washington Post,* March 20, 2003, p. A1.

Chapter 2: Fighting from a Distance: The Air Force and Navy

28. Quoted in Carol J. Williams, "Airstrikes Rev Up Fighter Pilots," *Milwaukee Journal-Sentinel,* March 23, 2003, p. A13.

29. Quoted in Otto Kreisher, "Aircraft Carrier Continues Air Strikes," (Illinois) *State Journal Register,* March 23, 2003, p. 11.

30. Quoted in George Cahlink, "Navy Sings 'Happy Trails' to the Iraq War," *National Journal,* May 10, 2003, p. 1,484.

31. Quoted in M.L. Lyke, "Routine Governs, Especially During War," *Seattle Post-Intelligencer,* March 24, 2003. http://seattlepi.nwsource.com.

32. Quoted in Chris Barron, "The Crew of Bremerton-Based USS *Rainier* Continues to Work Hard, but Can't Wait to Get Home," (Baltimore, Maryland) *Sun,* March 12, 2003, p. B1.

33. Quoted in *The Age,* "The Man Who Pressed the Button to Start the War," March 22, 2003. www.theage.com.au/articles/2003/03/21/1047749941746.html.

34. Quoted in Lyndsey Layton, "High Above the Carnage, U.S. Pilots Insulated from the Realities of Their Targets," *Washington Post,* April 2, 2003, p. A1.

35. Augustino, interview.

36. Quoted in Sharon Cohen, "Two Air Force Captains Flew from the Heart of America to the Heart of Iraq on a Bombing Run Last Month," *San Diego Union-Tribune,* May 4, 2003, p. A3.

37. Marlin Mosley, interview with author, Milwaukee, WI, November 20, 2003.

38. John Geragotelis, "First Person Singular," *Journal of Electronic Defense,* July 2003, p. 74.

39. Quoted in Stephanie McCrummen, "Fighting the Enemy—Boredom," *Newsday,* March 12, 2003, p. A4.

40. Quoted in Lyke, "Routine Governs, Especially During War."

41. National Public Radio, interview with George Porretta, March 27, 2003. www.npr.org/news/specials/wardiaries/archives.html.

42. Quoted in Kendra Helmer, "Some USS *Gary* Sailors Say Being on a Frigate Beats Carrier Duty Any Day," *Stars and Stripes,* April 18, 2003. www.stripes.com.

43. Quoted in Helmer, "Some USS *Gary* Sailors Say Being on a Frigate Beats Carrier Duty Any Day."

44. Quoted in Eric Morath, "Young Sailor Serves by Staying Submerged," *Plain Dealer,* May 27, 2003, p. B1.

45. Quoted in Doug Hummel, "Willow Grove Hospital Corpman Serves at 'Tip of the Knife' on USNS *Comfort*," Naval Air Station Joint Reserve Base, Willow, www.news.navy.mil.

46. Tim Martz, interview with author, Milwaukee, WI, November 11, 2003.

Chapter 3: Ground Troops in the Iraq War

47. Quoted in Geoffrey Mohan, "What War Left Behind," *Pittsburgh Post-Gazette,* April 20, 2003, p. A-17.

48. Quoted in J.D. Heyman, "Wounded in Action: Michael Mead and His Buddies Vowed to Take Care of Each Other. War Put Their Friendship and Courage to the Test," *People Weekly,* April 14, 2003, p. 62.

49. Quoted in Nahal Toosi, "Sandstorm Stops Troops in Their Tracks," *Milwaukee Journal-Sentinel,* March 26, 2003, p. 1A.

50. Quoted in Kelly Brooks, "Area Firefighter Tells of Stint in Iraq," *Sarasota Herald Tribune,* April 26, 2003, p. B1.

51. Quoted in Art Harris, "Journals Reveal Love, Courage, Fear," *Atlanta Journal-Constitution,* April 6, 2003, p. F6.

52. Quoted in Rick Atkinson, "For Infantrymen, Hardships Are Many and Nothing Is Easy," *Washington Post,* April 7, 2003, p. A26.

53. Quoted in Carol Ann Alaimo, "Tucson Marines Face Harsh Desert," *Arizona Daily Star,* April 7, 2003, p. A1.

54. Quoted in Tony Perry, "Combat's Lull a Pain in the Leatherneck," *Los Angeles Times,* March 30, 2003, p. A6.

55. Quoted in Doug Mellgren, "A Corporal from Kenosha Sees Shots Being Fired at His Unit, Then He Kills the Iraqi Soldier," *Wisconsin State Journal,* March 23, 2003, p. A6.

56. Quoted in Robinson, "The Insurgent and the Soldier," p. 50.

57. Quoted in Ellen Knickmeyer, "Marine Firepower Makes Strong Impression," Associated Press, April 2, 2003, in *NewsBank Special Report: Postwar Iraq.* www.infoweb.newsbank.com.

58. Quoted in Peter Baker, "A 'Turkey Shoot,' but with Marines as the Targets," *Washington Post,* March 27, 2003, p. A1.

59. Quoted in Craig Zentkovich, "Raiders Take Saddam International," April 10, 2003. www.centcom.mil/CENTCOM News/Stories/04_03/10.html.

60. Quoted in Simon Robinson, "Into the Fire with Warrior McCoy," *Time,* April 14, 2003, p. 62.

61. Quoted in Joseph B. Verrengia, "Battle Scars: Killing May Take Toll on Soldiers," *Milwaukee Journal-Sentinel*, April 20, 2003, p. 12A.

62. Quoted in Gordon Dillow, "Battle Transforms Fresh-Faced Troops," *Orange County Register*, March 23, 2003, p. 1.

63. Quoted in Liewer, "Wounded Soldiers Recount Harried Moments on the Battlefield."

64. Quoted in Kevin Peraino and Evan Thomas, "The Grunts' War," *Newsweek*, April 14, 2003, p. 32.

65. Quoted in Harris, "Journals Reveal Love, Courage, Fear," p. F6.

66. Quoted in Mohan, "What War Left Behind," p. A-17.

67. Quoted in Thomas Caywood, "Liberated POWs Describe Harrowing Captivity," *Boston Herald*, April 14, 2003, p. 4.

68. Quoted in Donna Miles, "Former POW Learns Value of Military Training," American Forces Press Service, October 8, 2003. www.defenselink.mil/news/Oct2003.

69. Quoted in Caywood, "Liberated POWs Describe Harrowing Captivity," p. 4.

70. Quoted in Bob Dart, "Wounded Warrior Fights to Heal," *Atlanta Journal-Constitution*, May 26, 2003, p. A3.

Chapter 4: U.S. Soldiers Help Rebuild Iraq

71. Quoted in Juliana Gittler, "Civil Affairs Helps Local Iraqis Recover from War, Looting," *Stars and Stripes*, August 24, 2003. www.stripes.com.

72. Quoted in Gittler, "Civil Affairs Helps Local Iraqis Recover from War, Looting."

73. Quoted in Michael Coronado, "Marines Help Feed Iraqis," (Riverside, California) *Press-Enterprise*, April 10, 2003, p. A18.

74. Quoted in Shawn C. Rhodes, "Marines Help Improve Lives," Central Command news release, April 19, 2003. www.centcom.mil/CENTCOMNews/Stories.

75. Quoted in Terry McCarthy, "Enter the Cleanup Crew," *Time*, March 24, 2003, p. 34.

76. Quoted in Associated Press, "Morale Wilts in Desert Heat, Combat Soldiers Ready for Home, Not Peacekeeping," *Charleston Daily Mail*, May 28, 2003, p. 5A.

77. Quoted in *Agence France-Presse*, "US Forces Assist Iraqi Town with First Election," April 28, 2003, in *NewsBank Special Report: Postwar Iraq*. www.infoweb.newsbank.com.

78. Quoted in Mark Brown, "96 Civil Affairs Fighting the Whole War in Western Iraq," Central Command news release, April 5, 2003. www.centcom.mil/CENTCOMNews/Stories.

79. Hartje, interview.

80. Quoted in Gittler, "Civil Affairs Helps Local Iraqis Recover from War, Looting."

81. Quoted in Ned Parker, "US Soldiers Go from Playing Rambo to Being Wall Street Wizards," *Agence France-Presse*, August 19, 2003. www.infoweb.newsbank.com.

82. Quoted in Meg Jones, "Starting with the Basics, Police Rebuild a Sharper, Fairer Iraq Force," *Milwaukee Journal-Sentinel*, December 28, 2003, p. 2B.

83. Quoted in Tini Tran, "GIs Work on Reconstruction in Iraq," Associated Press, October 16, 2003, in *NewsBank Special Report: Postwar Iraq*. www.infoweb.newsbank.com.

84. Daniel, interview.

85. Quoted in Nahal Toosi, "Platteville Soldier Killed by Bomb," *Milwaukee Journal-Sentinel*, December 27, 2003, p. 1A.

Chapter 5: A Constant Threat of Attack

86. L. Paul Bremer III, U.S. Department of Defense news transcript, December 14, 2003. www.defenselink.mil/transcripts/2003/tr20031214-1021.html.

87. Quoted in Kathleen T. Rhem, "Saddam Hussein 'Caught Like a Rat,' U.S. Commander Says," American Forces Press Service, December 14, 2003. www.defenselink.mil/news/Dec2003.

88. Quoted in Patrick J. McDonnell, "American Troops in Iraq Find It Difficult to Adapt to an Uneasy Peace," *Los Angeles Times*, July 5, 2003, p. 9A.

89. Quoted in Romesh Ratnesar, "Sticking to His Guns," *Time*, April 7, 2003, p. 36.

90. Quoted in Kimberly Hefling, "U.S. Pilots Learn Lessons in Urban Combat," Associated Press, April 3, 2003, in *NewsBank Special Report: Postwar Iraq*. www.infoweb.newsbank.com.

91. Quoted in Kevin Peraino, "Who Do You Trust?" *Newsweek*, April 7, 2003, p. 31.

92. Quoted in Ratnesar, "Sticking to His Guns."

93. Quoted in Nahal Toosi, "Soldiers Wary of Iraqi Civilians," *Milwaukee Journal-Sentinel*, April 5, 2003, p. 11A.

94. Quoted in Mohan, "What War Left Behind," p. A-17.

95. Quoted in John F. Burns, "A Pull of the Trigger, a Family's Changed Life," *International Herald Tribune*, April 14, 2003, p. 4.

96. Quoted in Alexandra Zavis, "Marines Carry Away Memories of Iraqis," Associated Press, April 23, 2003, in *NewsBank Special Report: Postwar Iraq*. www.infoweb.newsbank.com.

97. Quoted in Ned Parker, "US Soldiers Grouse over Lengthy Stays in Iraq," *Agence France-Presse*, July 18, 2003. www.infoweb.newsbank.com.

98. Quoted in Johanna McGeary, "Danger Around Every Corner," *Time*, October 20, 2003, p. 26.

99. Quoted in Eric Schmitt, "Soldiers Take Pride in Iraqi War Efforts but Think U.S. Will Be There Awhile," *Milwaukee Journal-Sentinel*, January 4, 2004, p. 1A.

100. Gregory Sielepkowski, interview with author, Milwaukee, WI, December 12, 2003.

101. Quoted in Chad D. Wilkerson, "Soldiers Renovate Day Care Center in Iraq," American Forces Press Service, October 30, 2003. www.defenselink.mil/news/Oct2003.

102. Quoted in Gina Cavallaro, "Soldiers Recount Moments After Crash," *Marine Times*, November 3, 2003. www.marinetimes.com.

103. Quoted in Tini Tran, "Non-Combat Troops Under Fire in Iraq War," *Milwaukee Journal-Sentinel*, October 26, 2003, p. 6A.

104. Quoted in Tran, "Non-Combat Troops Under Fire in Iraq War," p. 6A.

105. Martz, interview.

106. Quoted in Alan Bavley, "New Gear, Faster Response Saving More Soldiers' Lives," *Milwaukee Journal-Sentinel*, December 21, 2003, p. 3A.

107. Quoted in McGeary, "Danger Around Every Corner," p. 26.

108. Quoted in Patrick Quinn, "Night Raids a Staple in Saddam's Hometown," Associated Press, October 6, 2003, in *NewsBank Special Report: Postwar Iraq*. www.infoweb.newsbank.com.

109. Quoted in Quinn, "Night Raids a Staple in Saddam's Hometown."

110. Quoted in Joshua Hammer, "Lord . . . Just Help Us Kill 'Em," *Newsweek*, November 10, 2003, p. 19.

111. Quoted in John F. Burns, "Soldiers Nearly Lobbed Grenade into Hole Before Hussein Emerged," *Denver Post*, December 16, 2003, p. 1A.

112. Quoted in David Bennett, "Long Search for Saddam Ends in Ironhorse's Backyard," *V Corps News*, December 16, 2003. www.vcorps.army.mil.

Chapter 6: Iraq: A Difficult Place to Serve

113. Quoted in Donna Miles, "Deployed Soldier Brings Christmas to Baghdad,"
American Forces Press Service, December 24, 2003. www.defenselink.mil/news/Dec2003.

114. Quoted in Miles, "Deployed Soldier Brings Christmas to Baghdad."

115. Quoted in Simon Robinson, "At Tahir," *Time*, March 7, 2003, p. 46.

116. Daniel, interview.

117. Quoted in Petersi Liu, "Life Gets Better for Soldiers in Southern Iraq," *Defend America News*. October 3, 2003. www.defendamerica.mil.

118. Louis A. Arana-Barradas, "Adios Bashur (Airman's Notebook)," *Airman*, August 2003, p. 48.

119. Quoted in Thomas E. Ricks, "Comfort Rare in Iraq, Even for U.S. Troops," *Washington Post*, May 26, 2003, p. A1.

120. Sielepkowski, interview.

121. Martz, interview.

122. Gary Kernodle, interview with author, Milwaukee, WI, December 13, 2003.

123. Quoted in Kurt Pitzer, "Into the Fray: Fighting Fatigue, Nerves—and the Enemy—U.S. Forces Can Never Let Down Their Guard as They Relentlessly Press Forward," *People Weekly*, April 7, 2003, p. 54.

124. Quoted in Christian Caryl, "With the Ghost Squad: Mortar Attacks, Night Raids, Troubles Identifying Friend and Foe. On the Edge with Soldiers Fighting in the Gray Zone," *Newsweek*, November 17, 2003, p. 26.

125. Quoted in Amy Rinard, "Proud to Serve, but Sinking Under Debt," *Milwaukee*

Journal-Sentinel, December 21, 2003, p. 1A.

126. Quoted in Ann Scott Tyson, "Troop Morale in Iraq Hits 'Rock Bottom,'" *Christian Science Monitor,* July 7, 2003, p. 2.

127. Quoted in Shino Yuasa, "Tired and Depressed, GIs in Iraq Want to Go Home," *Agence France-Presse,* June 23, 2003, in *NewsBank Special Report: Postwar Iraq.* www.infoweb.newsbank.com.

128. Quoted in Marianne Szegedy-Maszak, "In Iraq, in Uniform, and in Turmoil," *U.S. News & World Report,* October 13, 2003, p. 46.

129. Quoted in Fiona O'Brien, "Soldiers Commit Suicide," *San Diego Union-Tribune,* October 23, 2003. www.signonsandiego.com.

130. Quoted in Wiley Hall, "'It's Good to Be Back,' Say Troops on Leave," *Grand Rapids Press,* September 26, 2003, p. A4.

131. Quoted in Laurel Walker, "Soldiers, Family Have Early Christmas," *Milwaukee Journal-Sentinel,* December 9, 2003, p. 2B.

132. Quoted in Tom Roeder, "Soldier Races Around World to Be at Son's Birth," (Colorado Springs) *Gazette,* November 8, 2003. www.gazette.com.

133. Quoted in Ron Hutcheson and Sudarsan Raghavan, "Bush Visits GIs in Iraq," *Milwaukee Journal-Sentinel,* November 28, 2003, p. 1A.

Epilogue: The Iraq War Changes Their Lives Forever

134. Quoted in Meg Jones, "Young Soldier Is Reflective and Grateful," *Milwaukee Journal-Sentinel,* December 28, 2003, p. 2B.

135. National Public Radio, interview with Ken Brown, April 9, 2003. www.npr.org/news/specials/wardiaries/archives.html.

136. Quoted in Zamira Eshanova, "Iraq: U.S. Soldiers in Baghdad Talk of Their Fears, Accomplishments, and Nightmares," Radio Free Europe, May 12, 2003. www.rferl.org/nca/features/2003/05/12052003155755.

137. Quoted in Joseph L. Galloway, "Healing the Wounds of War," *Knight Ridder Newspapers,* August 21, 2003. www.realcities.com.

138. Quoted in Katherine M. Skiba, "Back on His Feet," *Milwaukee Journal-Sentinel,* October 5, 2003, p. L2.

139. Kirk Straseskie, "Text of Letter from Kirk Straseskie," *Milwaukee Journal-Sentinel,* May 28, 2003, p. 2B.

140. Quoted in Tim Hammond, "An Email from Iraq: Life in the Sandbox," sent to the author December 9, 2003, after Hammond returned home.

★ For Further Reading ★

Books

Walter J. Boyne, *Operation Iraqi Freedom: What Went Right, What Went Wrong, and Why.* New York: Forge, 2003. A retired air force pilot turned military historian examines the war's military tactics.

Anthony H. Cordesman, *Iraq War: Strategy, Tactics, and Military Lessons.* New York: Greenwood, 2003. An overview of the Iraq War by a national security strategist at the Center for Strategic and International Studies.

Marc Kusnetz, *Operation Iraqi Freedom: The Inside Story.* Kansas City, MO: Andrews McMeel, 2003. This book explains how electronic journalists from NBC News reported the war.

Micah L. Sifry and Christopher Cerf, eds., *The Iraq War Reader: History, Documents, Opinions.* New York: Touchstone Books, 2003. A wide-ranging look at the Iraq War from many sources.

Murray Williamson and Robert H. Scales Jr., *The Iraq War: A Military History.* New York: Belknap Press, 2003. Two military historians explain combat in the Iraq War from a broader viewpoint than experiences of individual soldiers.

Jeff C. Young, *Operation Iraqi Freedom.* Berkeley Heights, NJ: Enslow, 2003. An overview of the Iraq War.

Karl Zinsmeister, *Boots on the Ground: A Month with the 82nd Airborne in the Battle for Iraq.* New York: Truman Talley Books, 2003. A reporter embedded with the 82nd Airborne Division gives a lively inside look at the life of soldiers.

Web Sites

Defend America (www.defendamerica.mil). The U.S. Department of Defense Internet site on the Iraq War and the war on terrorism.

Department of Defense (www.defenselink.mil). The U.S. Department of Defense Internet site on all military matters.

U.S. Central Command (www.centcom.mil). The official Internet site of the Central Command, the military group directing operations in Iraq.

☆ Works Consulted ☆

Books

Rick Bragg, *I Am a Soldier Too: The Jessica Lynch Story.* New York: Alfred A. Knopf, 2003. A former *New York Times* reporter recounts the experiences of Jessica Lynch in dramatic fashion.

Bing West and Ray L. Smith, *The March Up: Taking Baghdad with the 1st Marine Division.* New York: Bantam Books, 2003. Two retired military officers explain what it was like to accompany marines in the first weeks of the war.

Periodicals

Carol Ann Alaimo, "Tucson Marines Face Harsh Desert," *Arizona Daily Star,* April 7, 2003.

Louis A. Arana-Barradas, "Adios Bashur (Airman's Notebook)," *Airman,* August 2003.

Associated Press, "Morale Wilts in Desert Heat, Combat Soldiers Ready for Home, Not Peacekeeping," *Charleston Daily Mail,* May 28, 2003.

Rick Atkinson, "For Infantrymen, Hardships Are Many and Nothing Is Easy," *Washington Post,* April 7, 2003.

Peter Baker, "Marines Suit Up in Heavy, Hot Gear," *Washington Post,* March 15, 2003.

———, "A 'Turkey Shoot,' but with Marines as the Targets," *Washington Post,* March 27, 2003.

Julian E. Barnes, "Losing Pfc. Brown," *U.S. News & World Report,* April 28, 2003.

Chris Barron, "The Crew of Bremerton-Based USS *Rainier* Continues to Work Hard, but Can't Wait to Get Home," (Baltimore, Maryland) *Sun,* March 12, 2003.

Alan Bavley, "New Gear, Faster Response Saving More Soldiers' Lives," *Milwaukee Journal-Sentinel,* December 21, 2003.

Kelly Brooks, "Area Firefighter Tells of Stint in Iraq," *Sarasota Herald Tribune,* April 26, 2003.

John F. Burns, "A Pull of the Trigger, a Family's Changed Life," *International Herald Tribune,* April 14, 2003.

———, "Soldiers Nearly Lobbed Grenade into Hole Before Hussein Emerged," *Denver Post,* December 16, 2003.

George Cahlink, "Navy Sings 'Happy Trails' to the Iraq War," *National Journal,* May 10, 2003.

Christian Caryl, "With the Ghost Squad: Mortar Attacks, Night Raids, Troubles Identifying Friend and Foe. On the Edge with Soldiers Fighting in the Gray Zone," *Newsweek,* November 17, 2003.

Thomas Caywood, "Liberated POWs Describe Harrowing Captivity," *Boston Herald,* April 14, 2003.

Sharon Cohen, "Two Air Force Captains Flew from the Heart of America to the

Heart of Iraq on a Bombing Run Last Month," *San Diego Union-Tribune*, May 4, 2003.

Michael Coronado, "Marines Help Feed Iraqis," (Riverside, California) *Press-Enterprise*, April 10, 2003.

Bob Dart, "Wounded Warrior Fights to Heal," *Atlanta Journal-Constitution*, May 26, 2003.

Gordon Dillow, "Battle Transforms Fresh-Faced Troops," *Orange County Register*, March 23, 2003.

David Finkel, "Relief Comes in Bag of Skittles, U.S. Aid Convoys Move into Iraq," *Washington Post*, March 27, 2003.

John Geragotelis, "First Person Singular," *Journal of Electronic Defense*, July 2003.

Nancy Gibbs, "An American Family Goes to War," *Time*, March 24, 2003.

———, "Moving Out," *Time*, January 27, 2003.

Nancy Gibbs and Richard Stengel, "Oh God, Help Me Get Through It," *Time*, November 17, 2003.

Wiley Hall, "'It's Good to Be Back,' Say Troops on Leave," *Grand Rapids Press*, September 26, 2003.

Joshua Hammer, "Lord . . . Just Help Us Kill 'Em," *Newsweek*, November 10, 2003.

Art Harris, "Journals Reveal Love, Courage, Fear," *Atlanta Journal-Constitution*, April 6, 2003.

J.D. Heyman, "Wounded in Action: Michael Mead and His Buddies Vowed to Take Care of Each Other. War Put Their Friendship and Courage to the Test," *People Weekly*, April 14, 2003.

Ron Hutcheson and Sudarsan Raghavan, "Bush Visits GIs in Iraq," *Milwaukee Journal-Sentinel*, November 28, 2003.

Meg Jones, "Starting with the Basics, Police Rebuild a Sharper, Fairer Iraq Force," *Milwaukee Journal-Sentinel*, December 28, 2003.

———, "Young Soldier Is Reflective and Grateful," *Milwaukee Journal-Sentinel*, December 28, 2003.

Otto Kreisher, "Aircraft Carrier Continues Air Strikes," (Illinois) *State Journal Register*, March 23, 2003.

Lyndsey Layton, "High Above the Carnage, U.S. Pilots Insulated from the Realities of Their Targets," *Washington Post*, April 2, 2003.

Jessica Lynch, "Wrong Turn in the Desert," *Time*, November 17, 2003.

Ron Martz, "Troops Sense War Near," *Atlanta Journal-Constitution*, March 13, 2003.

Terry McCarthy, "Enter the Cleanup Crew," *Time*, March 24, 2003.

Stephanie McCrummen, "Fighting the Enemy—Boredom," *Newsday*, March 12, 2003.

Patrick J. McDonnell, "American Troops in Iraq Find It Difficult to Adapt to an Uneasy Peace," *Los Angeles Times*, July 5, 2003.

Johanna McGeary, "Danger Around Every Corner" *Time*, October 20, 2003.

Doug Mellgren, "A Corporal from Kenosha Sees Shots Being Fired at His Unit, Then He Kills the Iraqi Soldier," *Wisconsin State Journal*, March 23, 2003.

Geoffrey Mohan, "What War Left Behind," *Pittsburgh Post-Gazette*, April 20, 2003.

Eric Morath, "Young Sailor Serves by Staying Submerged," *Plain Dealer*, May 27, 2003.

Laura Coleman Noeth, "If War Is Hell, So Is Separation," *Commercial Appeal*, January 27, 2003.

Kevin Peraino, "Who Do You Trust?" *Newsweek*, April 7, 2003.

Kevin Peraino and Evan Thomas, "The Grunts' War," *Newsweek*, April 14, 2003.

Tony Perry, "Combat's Lull a Pain in the Leatherneck," *Los Angeles Times*, March 30, 2003.

Kurt Pitzer, "Into the Fray: Fighting Fatigue, Nerves—and the Enemy—U.S. Forces Can Never Let Down Their Guard as They Relentlessly Press Forward," *People Weekly*, April 7, 2003.

Romesh Ratnesar "Sticking to His Guns," *Time*, April 7, 2003.

Rick Reilly, "War Games," *Sports Illustrated*, October 28, 2003.

Thomas E. Ricks, "Comfort Rare in Iraq, Even for U.S. Troops," *Washington Post*, May 26, 2003.

Amy Rinard, "Proud to Serve, but Sinking Under Debt," *Milwaukee Journal-Sentinel*, December 21, 2003.

Kit T. Roane, "Dug In Far from Home," *U.S. News & World Report*, March 10, 2003.

Simon Robinson, "Basra," *Time*, March 31, 2003.

———, "Into the Fire with Warrior McCoy," *Time*, April 14, 2003.

———, "The Insurgent and the Soldier," *Time*, November 17, 2003.

———, "At Tahir," *Time*, March 7, 2003.

Roger Roy, "Delays Burden Marines in Kuwait," *Orlando Sentinel*, March 14, 2003.

Eric Schmitt, "Soldiers Take Pride in Iraqi War Efforts but Think U.S. Will Be There Awhile," *Milwaukee Journal-Sentinel*, January 4, 2004.

Mary Beth Sheridan, "This Is the Real Live Stuff, Ladies," *Washington Post*, March 20, 2003.

Katherine M. Skiba, "Back on His Feet," *Milwaukee Journal-Sentinel*, October 5, 2003.

Kirk Straseskie, "Text of Letter from Kirk Straseskie," *Milwaukee Journal-Sentinel*, May 28, 2003.

Marianne Szegedy-Maszak, "In Iraq, in Uniform, and in Turmoil," *U.S. News & World Report*, October 13, 2003.

Evan Thomas, "Fear at the Front," *Newsweek*, February 3, 2003.

Nahal Toosi, "Platteville Soldier Killed by Bomb," *Milwaukee Journal-Sentinel*, December 27, 2003.

———, "Reading, Writing, and Waiting for War," *Milwaukee Journal-Sentinel*, March 14, 2003.

———, "Sandstorm Stops Troops in Their Tracks," *Milwaukee Journal-Sentinel*, March 26, 2003.

———, "Soldiers Wary of Iraqi Civilians," *Milwaukee Journal-Sentinel*, April 5, 2003.

Tini Tran "Non-Combat Troops Under Fire in Iraq War," *Milwaukee Journal-Sentinel*, October 26, 2003.

Ann Scott Tyson, "Sands of Time Pass Slowly for Soldiers Poised in Kuwait," *Christian Science Monitor*, March 13, 2003.

———, "Troop Morale in Iraq Hits 'Rock Bottom,'" *Christian Science Monitor,* July 7, 2003.

Joseph B. Verrengia, "Battle Scars: Killing May Take Toll on Soldiers," *Milwaukee Journal-Sentinel,* April 20, 2003.

Laurel Walker, "Soldiers, Family Have Early Christmas," *Milwaukee Journal-Sentinel,* December 9, 2003.

Carol J. Williams, "Airstrikes Rev Up Fighter Pilots," *Milwaukee Journal-Sentinel,* March 23, 2003.

York Daily Record, "Hellam Woman Tells of Life at Sea in Wartime," May 26, 2003.

David Zucchino, "Soldiers Stumble on Outrageous Fortune," *Los Angeles Times,* April 19, 2003.

Internet Sources

The Age, "The Man Who Pressed the Button to Start the War," March 22, 2003. www.theage.com.au/articles/2003/03/21/1047749941746.html.

Agence France-Presse, "US forces Assist Iraqi Town with First Election," April 28, 2003, in *NewsBank Special Report: Postwar Iraq.* www.infoweb.newsbank.com.

Drew Brown, "Among the Infantry a Gritty, Hot Life with a Few Simple Pleasures," *Stars and Stripes,* March 19, 2003. www.stripes.com.

———, "On Eve of War, Infantrymen Wage Private Battles," *Stars and Stripes,* March 18, 2003. www.stripes.com.

Russ Bynum, "Troops Deploy from Across U.S. to Gulf," Associated Press, January 7, 2003, in *NewsBank Special Report: Postwar Iraq.* www.infoweb.newsbank.com.

Zamira Eshanova, "Iraq: U.S. Soldiers in Baghdad Talk of Their Fears, Accomplishments, and Nightmares," Radio Free Europe, May 12, 2003. www.rferl.org/nca/features/2003/05/12052003155755.

Federal News Service Inc., "B-1 Pilot Telephone Interviews," a transcript prepared for the U.S. Defense Department. www.defenselink.mil/transcripts/2003/tr20030408-t408phin.html.

Joseph L. Galloway, "Healing the Wounds of War," *Knight Ridder Newspapers,* August 21, 2003, www.realcities.com.

Juliana Gittler, "Civil Affairs Helps Local Iraqis Recover from War, Looting," *Stars and Stripes,* August 24, 2003. www.stripes.com.

Kimberly Hefling, "U.S. Pilots Learn Lessons in Urban Combat," Associated Press, April 3, 2003, in *NewsBank Special Report: Postwar Iraq.* www.infoweb.newsbank.com.

Kendra Helmer, "Dust Storms on the Waters," *Stars and Stripes,* March 17, 2003. www.stripes.com.

———, "Some USS *Gary* Sailors Say Being on a Frigate Beats Carrier Duty Any Day," *Stars and Stripes,* April 18, 2003. www.stripes.com.

Ellen Knickmeyer, "Marine Firepower Makes Strong Impression," Associated Press, April 2, 2003, in *NewsBank Special Report: Postwar Iraq.* www.infoweb.newsbank.com.

Steve Liewer, "Wounded Soldiers Recount Harried Moments on the Battlefield," *Stars and Stripes,* April 10, 2003. www.stripes.com.

M.L. Lyke, "Routine Governs, Especially During War," *Seattle Post-Intelligencer,* March 24, 2003. http://seattlepi.nwsource.com.

National Public Radio, interview with George Porretta, March 27, 2003. www.npr.org/news/specials/wardiaries/archives.html.

———, interview with Ken Brown, April 9, 2003. www.npr.org/news/specials/wardiaries/archives.html.

Fiona O'Brien, "Soldiers Commit Suicide," *San Diego Union-Tribune,* October 23, 2003. www.signonsandiego.com.

Mark Oliva, "Iraq War: Making History, Making Marines," *Stars and Stripes,* May 27, 2003. www.stripes.com.

———, "Marines Run Formation Drills to Refresh Essential Skills," *Stars and Stripes,* March 20, 2003. www.stripes.com.

Ned Parker, "US Soldiers Go from Playing Rambo to Being Wall Street Wizards," *Agence France-Presse,* August 19, 2003. www.infoweb.newsbank.com.

———, "US Soldiers Grouse over Lengthy Stays in Iraq," *Agence France-Presse,* July 18, 2003. www.infoweb.newsbank.com.

Patrick Quinn, "Night Raids a Staple in Saddam's Hometown," Associated Press, October 6, 2003, in *NewsBank Special Report: Postwar Iraq.* www.infoweb.newsbank.com.

Tom Roeder, "Soldier Races Around World to Be at Son's Birth," (Colorado Springs) *Gazette,* November 8, 2003. www.gazette.com.

Rick Scavetta, "American Troops Keep the Peace During a Typical Shift in 'the Bag,'" *Stars and Stripes,* July 6, 2003. www.stripes.com.

Tini Tran, "GIs Work on Reconstruction in Iraq," Associated Press, October 16, 2003, in *NewsBank Special Report: Postwar Iraq.* www.infoweb.newsbank.com.

Shino Yuasa, "Tired and Depressed, GIs in Iraq Want to Go Home," *Agence France-Presse,* June 23, 2003, in *NewsBank Special Report: Postwar Iraq.* www.infoweb.newsbank.com.

Alexandra Zavis, "Marines Carry Away Memories of Iraqis," Associated Press, April 23, 2003, in *NewsBank Special Report: Postwar Iraq.* www.infoweb.newsbank.com.

Military News Releases

David Bennett, "Long Search for Saddam Ends in Ironhorse's Backyard," *V Corps News,* December 16, 2003. www.vcorps.army.mil.

L. Paul Bremer III, U.S. Department of Defense news transcript, December 14, 2003. www.defenselink.mil/transcripts/2003/tr20031214-1021.html.

Mark Brown, "96 Civil Affairs Fighting the Whole War in Western Iraq," Central Command news release, April 5, 2003. www.centcom.mil/CENTCOMNews/Stories.

Gina Cavallaro, "Soldiers Recount Moments After Crash," *Marine Times,* November 3, 2003. www.marinetimes.com.

Miki Kristina Gilloon, "Canine Defenders Keep Warfighters Safe," U.S. Air Force news release, September 9, 2003. www.defendamerica.mil.

Doug Hummel, "Willow Grove Hospital Corpman Serves at 'Tip of the Knife' on USNS *Comfort,*" Naval Air Station Joint Reserve Base, Willow, www.news.navy.mil.

Petersi Liu, "Life Gets Better for Soldiers in Southern Iraq," *Defend America News.* www.defendamerica.mil.

Art Messer, "The Straight Scoop: A Seabee's Firsthand Account of Life in Iraq," e-mails

Messer sent home to American Legion Post 45. www.defendamerica.mil/articles/aug2003/a080703c.html.

Donna Miles, "Deployed Soldier Brings Christmas to Baghdad," American Forces Press Service, December 24, 2003. www.defenselink.mil/news/Dec2003.

———, "Former POW Learns Value of Military Training," American Forces Press Service, October 2003. www.defenselink.mil/news/Oct2003.

John Norgren, "Airman Witnesses Deadly Attack," U.S. Air Force news release, October 31, 2003. www.af.mil/stories.

Don Perrien, "Troops Deliver Child in Tallil Tent City," U.S. Air Force news release, October 31, 2003. www.af.mil/stories.

Todd Pruden, "Soldier Conducts Toy Drive for Iraqi Children," Armed Forces Press Service, October 28, 2003. www.defenselink.mil/news/Oct2003.

Kathleen T. Rhem, "Saddam Hussein 'Caught Like a Rat,' U.S. Commander Says," American Forces Press Service, December 14, 2003. www.defenselink.mil/news/Dec2003.

Shawn C. Rhodes, "Marines Help Improve Lives," Central Command news release, April 19, 2003. www.centcom.mil/CENTCOMNews/Stories.

Katherine Robinson, "Civil Affairs Soldiers Reach Out to Locals," Central Command news release, April 3, 2003. www.centcom.mil/CENTCOMNews/Stories.

———, "Military Lawyers Give Iraqi Courts a Helping Hand," June 24, 2003. www.defendamerica.mil/articles.

Ricardo Sanchez, Coalition Provisional Authority press briefing, November 11, 2003. Transcript by Federal News Service Inc. www.centcom.mil/CentcomNews/Transcripts/20031101.htm.

Larry Stevens, "Mother of Six Serves as Operation Iraqi Freedom Truck Driver," October 31, 2003. www.defenselink.mil/news/Oct2003.

Jeremy M. Vought, "Food on the Go!" 1st Force Service Support Group, March 4, 2003. www.usmc.mil.

———, "Rodeo Kicks Up Sand in Kuwaiti Desert," 1st Force Service Support Group, March 23, 2003. www.usmc.mil.

Chad D. Wilkerson, "Soldiers Renovate Day Care Center in Iraq," American Forces Press Service, October 30, 2003. www.defenselink.mil/news/Oct2003.

———, "U.S. Army Delivers Soccer Balls to Northern Iraq," July 27, 2003. www.defendamerica.mil/articles.

Leonard Wong et al., "Why They Fight: Combat Motivation in the Iraq War," Strategic Studies Institute, July 2003. www.army.mil/prof_writing/volumes/volume1/september_2003/9_03_1.html.

Craig Zentkovich, "Raiders Take Saddam International," April 10, 2003. www.centcom.mil/CENTCOMNews/Stories/04_03/10.html.

☆ Index ☆

★ Picture Credits ★

Cover: Shawn Baldwin/EPA/Landov
Ali Abbas/EPA/Landov, 65
AP/Wide World Photos, 75
Department of Defense, 70
Ali Jasim/Reuters/Landov, 67
Joe Raedle/Getty Images, 45
Cpl. Jeff Sisto/U.S. Marine Corps, 63
UPI/Landov, 47
U.S. Air Force photo by Staff Sgt. Aaron
    Allmon II, 54
U.S. Air Force photo by Staff Sgt.
    Reynaldo Ramon, 82
U.S. Air Force photo by Staff Sgt. Cherie
    A. Thurlby, 85
U.S. Navy photo, 29
U.S. Navy photo by Chief Journalist Alan
    J. Baribeau, 34
U.S. Navy photo by Journalist 1st
    Class Greg Cleghorne, 12

U.S. Navy photo by Journalist 1st Class
    Joseph Krypel, 21
U.S. Navy photo by Photographer's
    Mate 1st Class Arlo K. Abrahamson,
    50, 76
U.S. Navy photo by Photographer's
    Mate 1st Class Shane T. McCoy, 35
U.S. Navy photo by Photographer's
    Mate 2nd Class Jacob A. Johnson,
    53
U.S. Navy photo by Photographer's
    Mate 2nd Class Michael Sandberg,
    79
U.S. Navy photo by Photographer's
    Mate 3rd Class Michael S. Kelly, 31
Lance Cpl. Brian L. Wickliffe/U.S.
    Marine Corps, 41
Jamal A. Wilson/EPA/Landov, 57
Steve Zmina, 19, 27

☆ About the Author ☆

Michael V. Uschan has written more than thirty books, including *The Korean War*, for which he won the 2002 Council of Wisconsin Writers Juvenile Nonfiction Award. Mr. Uschan began his career as a writer and editor with United Press International, a wire service that provides stories to newspapers, radio, and television. Journalism is sometimes called "history in a hurry." Mr. Uschan considers writing history books a natural extension of the skills he developed in his many years as a journalist. He and his wife, Barbara, reside in the Milwaukee suburb of Franklin, Wisconsin.